THE
HAPPY
SALES
MANAGER

THE HAPPY SALES MANAGER

Drive Sales, Lead Your Team with Ease, and Have Fun!

GRETCHEN GORDON

For more information, email ggordon@braveheartsales.com

ISBN: 979-8-88759-989-2 - paperback
ISBN: 979-8-89109-043-9 - hardcover
ISBN: 979-8-88759-991-5 - ebook
ISBN: 979-8-89109-295-2 - audiobook

Download the Workbook for Free!!

To get the best experience with this book and because I wanted to make it easy for you to apply what you read I am offering the companion workbook for FREE. I've found that readers who download and use *The Happy Sales Manager Workbook* can implement the suggestions in this book faster and take the next steps needed to become the best sales manager possible, while getting their life back and enjoying their job more.

You can get a copy by visiting:

http://www.thehappysalesmanager.com/

*To the dedicated Braveheart Sales Performance
team and the clients you serve,
Without all of you, this book would not exist.*

*To my family,
Thank you for supporting all the ideas I cook
up on my entrepreneurial journey.
(and we all know that is all I cook up)*

Contents

Introduction

You may be reading this book because you have never been a sales manager before and you are newly promoted. Or you want to become a sales manager. Or you have been a sales manager for a while and are seeking to make your job more enjoyable and more efficient. Whichever is your situation, congratulations on taking a step toward becoming the best sales manager you can become while enjoying the job.

I felt inspired to write this book because I landed my first sales leadership role only because I was an effective salesperson and had some natural executive presence. But I did not enjoy it. I didn't fully understand the sales manager's mission, and I didn't have guidance or coaching to help me succeed. So this book is designed mostly for those individuals who find themselves in a sales manager role where they are slightly unsure, maybe lacking confidence, and probably not enjoying the role. Additionally, it's for those that have been in sales management for a while and just want to enjoy it more and have more success.

Sales management is not for the weak of heart. It doesn't necessarily come naturally, it is different than general management, and it requires a variety of skills—a unique combination of coaching skills, motivational focus, and a discipline around holding others accountable to their required activities and behaviors. For the most part, these haven't been taught and companies rarely have it all laid out for the sales manager concerning performance metrics, how to spend their time, and the necessary skills to be world-class. So you may feel lost. You may not know exactly what to do to perform well in your role.

As the leader of the sales team, regardless of team size, it is your job to drive sales through your team to accomplish the financial goals of the company by growing revenue and profits. You are to help your team members grow and develop to the best of their abilities and become better at their role than they would be if you were not their leader. This is weighty stuff and, in some respects, selfless. You must put the team before yourself. You need to step out of the spotlight and shine it on your team. And these are far different skills than you may have used as a salesperson.

You may sometimes feel like the disciplinarian, sometimes like a friend, and sometimes like a babysitter. This is normal. Leading a sales team is messy. You have to balance the company's goals of driving results with the nuanced, unique, and complicated personalities that make up the sales team. Since effective salespeople are not clones of each other, there isn't a one-size-fits-all approach, so you must approach each individual on your team as an individual.

Let's begin the mission to help you become the best sales leader you can be and enjoy your job while doing it. To gain the most benefit from this book, download *The Happy Sales Manager Workbook*, which provides all the templates and exercises listed in the book and can be found at thehappysalesmanager.com.

Key Competencies to Master

While many aspects are needed to effectively accomplish a sales manager's mission, this first section will deal with the most important competencies that are required, not only for success but also enjoyment in the role. Any world-class sales manager should spend the vast majority of their time on them:

- Motivating and Goal Setting
- Accountability
- Coaching
- Recruiting

I suggest you start by understanding and embracing these core elements of your role discussed in this chapter. However, feel free to jump to other sections of the book if you need to explore a specific topic. But then come back to this part because it is critically important that you read and absorb these core elements of your role to have the greatest success in sales management. They are critically important not only for your success but also for your peace of mind.

Motivating and Goal Setting

"People often say that motivation doesn't last. Neither does bathing—that's why we recommend it daily."

—*Zig Ziglar*

As we embark on helping you execute your goal of excellence in sales leadership, one of the first requirements is to understand the role that motivation plays in the effectiveness of your team. Since it is important to have highly motivated salespeople on your team, understanding *how* they are motivated, not just that they *are* motivated, is critically important to help you inspire them and, therefore, help them produce the best results they can, day in and day out.

You might be thinking that it isn't your job to understand the motivational tendencies of your team, as it is their job to come to work motivated. You might even have a thought in the back of your head that salespeople who aren't motivated are weak and will fail, so maybe it is better to weed them out now. After all, you were likely pretty self-motivated to get the job done. That is probably what got you here. But the truth is while I fully support hiring highly motivated individuals, even the most motivated individuals need some help along the way in the motivation department. Sure you could just decide to hire only those that require little motivational guidance from you. But the problem is that you will have to spend a lot of time finding those individuals.

So it's best to accept the fact that you may have to insert yourself into the motivational process with your salespeople to help them stay on track.

Understanding what motivates the people on your team and tapping into that will make your job so much easier.

I will not suggest that one person can fully motivate another. That needs to come from within the person. But you can inspire them. The most effective sales managers understand how they can inspire salespeople and what each member responds to. They may all be different. Some people respond to praise and a thank you from their boss. Some respond to praise and accolades from their clients. Some need public recognition. Still others need rewards and money to motivate them. And then some need a swift kick in the rear to get them going. They need to be scolded for not doing what they should do before they will respond. I used to work with someone like this: he was extremely effective after a scolding. The boss knew that every once in a while he had to bring him in and give him a stern talking to and then the guy would light the world on fire.

Money isn't always motivating

It has been a widely held truth for as long as I can remember that salespeople are inherently money-motivated. And based on our interactions with hundreds of CEOs, most truly believe this. Unfortunately, many managers miss the boat by painting all salespeople with the same brush. They try to inspire salespeople by talking about the commission they will earn or, worse, by encouraging them to go buy an expensive car, believing that the pressure to make those car payments will universally turn them into a selling machine. This might work for some salespeople, but by and large, it won't work for most.

Speaking for myself (I am a baby boomer), while I didn't enter sales because of the money, I stayed because of it. Interestingly, though, that isn't what drives many salespeople today. Many salespeople are highly motivated yet are motivated by other elements instead of money. Let's take a closer look at the various motivation styles:

- **Extrinsic**—Motivated by money, rewards, toys, vacations, and material things. They are more effective in a shorter and/or more heavily commissioned sales cycle.
- **Intrinsic**—Motivated by recognition, fulfillment, satisfaction, enjoyment, love of selling, mastery, or even competition with others. They are often more consistent in a longer and more complex sales cycle.
- **Altruistic**—Motivated to serve others at a cost to themselves. They will put the customer ahead of their company's needs and requirements.

To illustrate my point that not all salespeople are money-motivated, I reviewed data on 25 companies we had analyzed over the last several months, which included 544 salespeople. I found the following statistics:

- 39 percent of the salespeople in these 25 companies were motivated by non-monetary or reward reasons (intrinsically motivated).
- 36 percent were motivated by money and rewards (extrinsically motivated).
- 7 percent were motivated by service to others (altruistically motivated).
- 18 percent were motivated by a combination of these.

These sales teams came from a wide variety of industries that sell a variety of products and services, so the numbers are very representative and not confined to one industry.

You may be thinking that your team is made up of all money-motivated, extrinsically driven salespeople. Fine. If that is your team, then you know how to inspire them. It just takes money. It is possible, though, that you only think they are money-motivated because they have told you they want to make the most money they can. Most anybody would like to make as much money as they can. So the question is not, do they want to make a lot of money, but rather, are they willing to do what it takes to maximize their earnings? In other words, is money enough to get them to do the difficult things? The time-consuming things? Will they go to the mat to drive results for the additional money? Maybe not. Of the 25 companies described above, only 9 of those companies had more extrinsically motivated salespeople than intrinsically. In my experience working with hundreds of frustrated leaders who have revamped their compensation plans to give monetary rewards to the sellers who crush their goals, money alone doesn't cause many salespeople to operate differently.

Remember that 61 percent of the salespeople in the sample were *not* motivated solely by money.

Intrinsically motivated salespeople don't necessarily respond well to traditional means of sales management. Instead of hearing how much more money they can make, this group requires more finesse and intimate management. Don't assume this group isn't as driven as their money-focused (extrinsically motivated) counterparts, though. You will just need to tap into different triggers. I also analyzed the level of motivation these salespeople possessed and found that across a wide variety of industries, intrinsically and extrinsically motivated salespeople had the same level of motivational drive. Most were highly driven. To be exact, 84 percent of them.

Other motivators

You might be wondering what might motivate a salesperson if not money. The following key drivers can be just as powerful to drive an intrinsically motivated seller as compensation does for those money-motivated souls.

- Praise and recognition
- Satisfaction
- Fulfillment
- Mastery of their role
- Love for what they do

If they are motivated by...	Things to say	Things to do
Praise and recognition	"Great job with that difficult account."	Praise them frequently for their efforts
Satisfaction in a job well done	"You should be so satisfied with your work with ABC Company."	Suggest a few hours away to bask in the success
Mastery of their role	"I have noticed a real improvement in your sales execution."	Offer additional training resources
Love of what they do	"I can see the joy coming out in your work."	Remove administrative distractions

How you utilize each type of motivator depends on the individual's preference for the following components:

- Loving to win vs. hating to lose
- Purchasing things to create pressure to pay for them vs. buying something as a reward only after making the sale
- Being pressured vs. self-pressure
- Being closely managed vs. self-management

- Competing against others vs. self-competition
- Recognition vs. satisfaction
- Having something to prove vs. not having something to prove

Understanding this about your team members can provide you with guidance on how to interact with the different sellers on your team. However, it isn't enough to just understand it. You must act on it by talking with everyone individually.

Example 1: Let's say you have two salespeople you need to motivate, as they each have a large opportunity they are working to close. One loves to win and one hates to lose. When coaching them through their upcoming sales conversations to try and win the business, it can be as simple as discussing with one their plan to win the business and with the other their plan to ensure they don't lose the business.

Example 2: In this example, you have one salesperson who is motivated by competing against others and another who is motivated by competing against themself. When coaching the individual who needs to compete against others, you must list where they stand in comparison to others and discuss ways they will "beat" their peers. With the self-competing individual, focus on how they will overcome their last month or quarter, or how you see them beating their best month ever in sales.

Example 3: If you have an individual who has something to prove, you are in luck. They are highly motivated. Maybe they were told they would never amount to anything. Maybe they dropped out of college and their parents are down on them. If they possess a chip on their shoulder, these individuals are generally very self-motivated, so you may just need to demonstrate that you are there to support them in their quest. Encourage them to conquer their demons. Unfortunately, if you have someone who does not have anything to prove, you will need to find something else within them that you can inspire.

It's amazing how tapping into motivators can spur an individual to excellence while making a sales manager's life so much easier.

Using goal setting

If you want to create a well-oiled machine of highly motivated producers, use the power of goal setting. I am not talking about doling out the sales goals or quotas for the year. I am talking about aiding each team member to establish their own personal goals related to what they want out of this world. Do they see themselves with more toys and a big house in the future? Do they see themselves slowing down in the next five years so they can have time to volunteer at their church? Whatever matters to them, you must tap into it. And do this for yourself too. What do you really want?

Here's how it works.

Get to know them. Start by getting to really know the people that report to you, not just for their sales ability, but also for who they are, what they care about, what bothers them, and how they see themselves. Sound hard? If you are like many sales managers, you may not feel comfortable getting that close to them. However, if you focus on the mission as it relates to your people—helping them achieve and get what they want—then it is easier. Don't view it as becoming buddies with them. View deepening the relationship as a way to understand what makes them tick, which therefore enlightens you on what you can do to help them excel. It isn't enough for you to do it for these reasons; the salesperson also has to feel like you are doing it for their benefit. They have to truly believe that you are interested in helping them achieve their goals.

Earn their trust. It may take time to prove that you are there for *them*, not just prying. You may need to earn their trust by showing up for them, encouraging them, or challenging them—whatever makes sense to connect with them. Perhaps you grab coffee with them individually and just talk about what they want to talk about. You may have to let your guard down and tell them something about yourself.

Whatever you do, you have to articulate that you are in their corner. You want them to succeed. But just saying it isn't enough. As they say, actions speak louder than words. Remember, connecting with your team members is not a one-size-fits-all approach. And those who are different from you in terms of personality and communication style may be more difficult to connect with.

Help them set goals. Once you have their trust that you are on their team, you can help walk them through the process of goal setting.

Step 1: Get them to really think about and picture their personal long-term goals. For instance, do they want to remodel their kitchen? Do they want to buy a vacation home? Do they want to donate more money to charity over the long haul?

Step 2: Have them then think more near term. What do they want this year? Is their remodeled kitchen a goal to accomplish this year or do they need to save money over a few years to accomplish that? How much money do they need to sock away this year to help them accomplish their longer term goals that are a few years in the making? Or how much do they need to realize their near term, current year goal?

Step 3: Help them determine a budget for their goals. Whatever they desire, get them to calculate the budget for what it will cost to accomplish these things or save for these things.

Step 4: Have them calculate their Math of Success. This will tie their goals to what they must do every day to achieve those goals. This calculation is mostly designed for those individuals that have some variable compensation component that is based on their sales production. To do this:

- Write down their sales goal for the year (their financial goals identified in Step 3. *Caveat: Their financial goal must meet or exceed the goal that the company needs them to produce, and in my experience, it almost always does.)
- Divide by 12 to get the monthly sales goal
- Determine their average sale size by dividing how many closed sales they had by the number of sales made (if they sell some very large items and some small, you may want to break this down into two separate calculations)
- Multiply their closing ratio (this ratio should be the percentage of opportunities they close from the number of discovery or first exploratory sales conversations they had with potential prospects, and if their closing ratio had not been tracked, make a guess and then start tracking it with the plan to adjust once there is some history)
- This should indicate the number of first-discovery meetings or exploratory sales conversations they need to have every month, and if a month feels too long, divide this number by 4.35 to determine the number they need each week

The beauty of the Math of Success is that numbers do not lie. Whether they need one discovery meeting a week or 20, this number is based on their data. If they want to conduct fewer first meetings, then they either need to increase the size of the sales opportunities they pursue or improve their closing ratio.

Step 5: Now they must identify specifically and measurably what they will do each week to reach their prescribed number of first meetings per week or month. This is where the rubber meets the road and is where the magic happens. You may need to help them brainstorm what those activities could be. If they are completely reliant on the leads that your marketing generates, this will not work. If you feel like you must supply them with all the leads they could ever want, this will not work. This part of the planning process is designed to shift responsibility from leadership and marketing to the salesperson. I am not saying don't provide leads to them. I am saying, you need to make them aware that they must do something to accomplish their goals. And, remember, if they come up with activities that you know will not support their goals, you must assert your veto power, keeping in mind that you are trying to help them accomplish their goals.

Step 6: Once agreed upon, you now have an action plan from each of your salespeople, and now, you must hold them accountable, using their roadmap. This is the hardest part of the process. Becoming their accountability partner by ensuring they do what they said they would do is not necessarily easy, but it is simple. Meet with them weekly. Ask if they did what they committed to from an activity standpoint. If they did not, simply ask, "What are you going to do differently next week to ensure success?" And since you know why they are doing the work, remind them that they might not be able to buy that boat or donate to charity the way they had planned. Frequent reminders of why they are doing this job are far more powerful than just telling them to do more.

The Happy Sales Manager Workbook, which can be found on our platform, thehappysalesmanager.com, includes a Sales Action Planning Playbook if you want a template to walk through the six steps above.

Adapt your coaching and how you inspire salespeople to go that extra mile by understanding how each is motivated, then be intentional with each individual to help them articulate their personal goals. It will make your life easier and your salespeople will be more successful.

KEY TAKEAWAYS

- Motivating is a key component of your role and is critical to your success.

- The discipline of goal setting is one of the most powerful tools you have at your discretion to help inspire individuals.

- Helping everyone on the team create their own Math of Success creates a sense of intimacy and ownership of a plan of attack for each individual.

- You must individualize how you approach motivation with each separate individual, which requires that you understand each team member personally.

Improvement Exercise: Schedule a meeting to introduce the Math of Success and have everyone construct their own. Be sure to provide oversight and guidance if their math doesn't work or they are off base.

Accountability

It might seem obvious to you that creating a plan of attack to accomplish the goals, then focusing on doing what will help you accomplish them is what you need to do. Unfortunately, this thought process is not necessarily inherent in all salespeople. They sometimes think by doing something, anything, they're progressing. But salespeople fail for only two reasons. The second one will be explored in the next chapter. The first is that they don't do enough of the *right* stuff.

So you need to hold them accountable to doing the right tasks that will help them complete their Math of Success. Frankly, it is a disservice if you don't hold them accountable. Salespeople can be distracted easily. And if they don't have you as their partner to help them stay on track with the things that will produce success, they can become wayward. You are letting them down if you don't nudge them to do what the math indicates will ensure success.

Focus on leading indicators, not just lagging indicators

We all know that the scorecard for sales reps is their closed business. But if we focus only on this *outcome* goal, we may end up putting too much pressure on the sales reps to perform, which may actually reduce their likelihood of success.

Yes, your team and each individual needs to hit their sales goal. However, they have absolutely no control over whether the prospect will buy anything, let alone from them. You must accept this fact. The salesperson cannot make a prospect buy from them. When managers constantly harp on the endgame, the closed business goal, without an appropriate amount of focus on the process goals, they place undue pressure on situations beyond the sales reps' control, thereby causing extra stress without providing much guidance on how to actually succeed. Now don't get me wrong; I am not opposed to a little stress. Sales reps should always have an appropriate dose of angst, causing them to complete the necessary activities to get the right opportunities in the pipeline. But just telling a salesperson to close more business is rarely effective. Unfortunately, in most companies, too much focus is placed on the sale, which is old, historic data, and not enough emphasis is placed on the everyday activities that reps should do to generate those opportunities.

Sales reps are like professional athletes in that they need to do the little things every day to ensure the highest likelihood of success. In sports psychology, they focus on the concept of process vs. outcome goals because the athlete cannot totally control the end result. It is a common practice to focus the athlete on the process or individual elements that lead to success as opposed to the outcome goal in order to reduce tension and improve performance. This is relevant for sales as well. If we can adjust our thinking to focus on the activity goals (number of attempts to reach prospects, number of requests for introductions, etc.) instead of the outcome goals (number of proposals or closed business), then the emphasis will be appropriately placed and will produce better outcome results (more quality proposals and more closed business). And the sales rep will feel less pressure during sales appointments. Remember, the sales rep does not have control of the outcome. And when they do not have control over the situation and are under pressure to produce the results, they will be under too much stress. Their brains will not work as effectively when under this kind of stress. So let's reduce the stress experienced by the sales rep in the selling situation to improve their brain function and their ability to produce a successful outcome.

Focus on the activity goals, not exclusively the outcome goals, and your reps will focus on the right behaviors, which, in turn, will produce more successful results.

When contemplating what those *right* activities are, refer back to the Math of Success, which we covered in chapter 1 and is available in *The Happy Sales Manager Workbook*, found at thehappysalesmanager.com and if you haven't had everyone on your team complete this work, do it now.

To really hold them accountable, you need to zero in on the right activities to produce first meetings. Just tracking the number of first meetings doesn't get to the heart of the matter. It is a starting point. But you could argue that first meetings are also a type of lagging indicator. They are the tipping point and a leading indicator for closed business, but they're really a lagging indicator of whether the individual has done enough of the right activities to produce those first meetings. So, if you really want to make your life easy and improve the efficiency of the team, get fanatical about them engaging in activities to produce those first meetings. Ignore their calls for more marketing. Ignore the request for better resources to target. Ignore their excuses as to why they cannot close more business and zero in on the actual activities they are doing every day to create new opportunities.

When they completed their Math of Success, they were prompted to identify what activities and the number of each activity they will commit to completing each week. And remember, you had veto power if their activities were unlikely to produce enough first meetings. So by now, you should have it set, and you are merely an accountability partner to hold them to their commitments. Rather than telling them what to do, you are a partner in their journey to success.

And if they aren't completing the activities they listed in their plan, simply ask them what they are going to do differently this week to ensure they get those activities done. Get specific with them. Drill down. Help them succeed. As part of their action plan, you could also ask them what consequences they will impose on themselves if they don't meet their activity goal each week. Likewise, I would suggest that they list some small rewards they will engage in when they do meet their activity goals each week.

The following three questions will help you determine what activity they must do and how many times they must do it to populate the pipeline with enough opportunities to produce success:

1. What is the most important activity that your salespeople can do that opens up an opportunity? In most selling situations, this is the initial discovery appointment where one determines whether they have a live opportunity or not.
2. What percentage of that activity leads to closed business for this salesperson?
3. How many new pieces of new business does the salesperson need to close?

Once you have the answers to these critical questions, it is time to get your team's buy-in. If the answers are accurate, all you need to do is focus on the number of times they do that important activity in the first question. For example, if salesperson *A* needs to close 24 new accounts during the year (two per month), and he closes 25 percent of discovery appointment opportunities, then he needs 96 discovery appointments over the course of the year, or 8 per month.

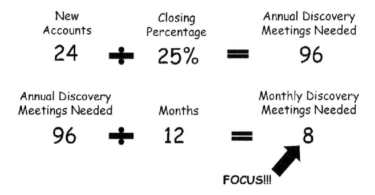

New Accounts		Closing Percentage		Annual Discovery Meetings Needed
24	÷	25%	=	96

Annual Discovery Meetings Needed		Months		Monthly Discovery Meetings Needed
96	÷	12	=	8

FOCUS!!!

Easy, peasy, lemon squeezy. Just focus your folks on doing the things that will enable them to conduct those eight quality discovery appointments per month. The closed business will take care of itself. If the closed business isn't coming, then that is a whole different issue that requires coaching intervention, which is covered in the next chapter.

Focus on discovery meetings

The reason I focus only on discovery meetings or first appointments in the calculation above is that in our initial focus on accountability, the number of total meetings doesn't matter. You see, some opportunities close in just one meeting. Some take 5 or even 10 or more meetings to close. You may have some idea of the typical number of meetings necessary to get a piece of business closed in your company, but that can come later as you are monitoring their closing success. If you first focus on the initial meeting and getting your team to zero in on the things they can do every single day to increase the number of initial meetings (not reliant on the company's marketing), that is half the battle. The Math of Success will calculate this for you.

So definitely track the number of discovery meetings everyone on the team has. If they are account managers without goals to attract new customers, then track the number of first discussions that they have with their existing clients about a new service. Again, use the Math of Success to determine what that needs to be for their individual situation. If you know how many first meetings each seller has, then it opens a whole new world of insight that can be beneficial, including:

- Each individual's closing ratio, which allows you to compare and contrast the team members' effectiveness in closing business—using first meetings as a starting point to calculate this ratio.
- Which team members aren't having enough first meetings, which can direct you to ask them what they are going to do to acquire their first meeting goal this week and going forward to ensure they have enough opportunities in their pipeline to accomplish their goals.
- Which team members have many first meetings but a lagging closing ratio, which signals they may need some coaching. It may be time to participate in some calls or sales meetings with them to identify the problem. Additionally, if they are responsible for generating their own leads, this may indicate they are fishing in the wrong pond. This provides an opportunity for you to redirect toward your target market and maybe revisit your company's value proposition and who benefits. It

may also indicate that they aren't very good at qualifying or disqualifying opportunities, which means you may need to intervene to help them build the disqualifying skill. Even if the company is generating marketing leads for them and you feel responsible to provide good leads, it is still ultimately the salesperson's responsibility to produce an adequate number of qualified opportunities. Whether their leads are good or bad, the salesperson is still responsible for the sales goal, and it begins with a first sales conversation.

A word about micromanaging

I have heard many sales managers say, "I don't want to be a micro-manager," and I agree. This sounds horrible. But holding them accountable is the exact opposite of micromanaging. Micromanaging is when you must tell your salespeople what to do each week or each day and when you must track every moment of their time. That is not what I am talking about. I am asking that you pay attention to the activities they do to produce first discovery meetings, as that will produce success.

This is not micromanaging. This is ensuring success. But you may have some salespeople that push back. They may say, "I've always met my goals. I don't need you breathing down my neck." Stay strong and assure them that it is for their own good, to make them the most efficient they can be to produce the most business they can and enjoy the rewards from doing so.

You must remember that it is far easier to address the expectations and establish these ground rules than to address them if a salesperson slips. Let's assume that you have a high-performing salesperson so you don't require their commitment to the Math of Success and the accompanying activity plan. And all is well. Except that at some point, their production falls off, and you don't even know where to begin to come to their aid. Do you think it is more difficult to address their decline at that point without any game plan, or would it have been easier to have a roadmap based on what they committed to do from an activity standpoint? The plan would at least allow you to know where to begin. Are they doing the activities they committed to? If not, that can be a super easy fix. If they are, then you also know where to help because they may need coaching. But without the plan derived from their Math of Success, you will be left fumbling around in the dark, trying to solve the issue.

The quicker you can diagnose the root cause of the lack of closings, the quicker you can follow the right path to help the salesperson correct and achieve success.

Sales manager accountability framework

Use this easy-to-follow checklist to help you kick off more intentional accountability practices. Some of this may seem basic, but the use of this checklist will ensure you have everyone focused correctly and will make your life easier throughout the year.

1. All individual salespeople must know your expectations of them regarding sales, including the source and type of sales:
   - New clients vs. expansion of existing clients or a combination thereof
   - Products or services mix desired
   - Average size of the sale
   - Acceptable profit margins (if they have price control)

If you take a bottom-up approach, just make certain everyone has completed their sales goal work and that it will produce enough business to help you meet your goals as a division. Generally, a bottom-up approach causes salespeople to identify a loftier goal than you would have assigned them, so I love this approach. Just make sure it is all in check.

2. Everyone has completed their own Math of Success, which should calculate how many first discovery meetings they need to fill the pipeline full of quality opportunities that predict success. The components necessary to construct an individual Math of Success are:

   - Monthly sales goal (annual goal divided by 12)
   - Average sale size (If a salesperson is responsible for a set of services or products that are wide-ranging in value, it may be appropriate to complete separate Math of Success calculations for each type. In most cases you will want to avoid a seller counting on one large opportunity closing.)
   - Closing ratio from first discovery meeting to closed business

By knowing these items, the salesperson can then construct the required number of first discovery meetings to achieve their sales goals. Focus only on first discovery meetings to consistently drive the right prospecting behaviors versus simply having a certain number of meetings.

3. As part of their Math of Success, everyone has created a Sales Action Plan. This is their commitment to doing the activities that will ensure they have enough first meetings as calculated by their Math of Success. Remember to have them set rewards and consequences.

The key is to have buy-in from them and that they own the plan and the consequences.

4. A regular one-on-one meeting cadence is set and agreed upon with each individual where you will review their adherence to their Sales Action Plan activities and a certain number of first discovery meetings. This should be *very* regular, as in weekly, unless your team sells exceptionally large services with exceptionally long sales cycles. However, remember that just because they sell big "stuff" and aren't selling many of them, they still need to always be focused on business expansion. So, you need to pay attention to some level of activity.

Excuses stop here

The beauty of this framework is that it will be much harder for salespeople to make excuses about their activities. When the focus is simply on sales outcomes, it's very easy to place blame on why the sales didn't occur (the economy, the competition, your company). But it is much harder to blame someone else when they didn't do what they had agreed upon. By being diligent about this process, your salespeople will have more clarity into what their actions produce, making them their own accountability partner.

However, a salesperson may still pull out one of their go-to excuses like, "I was busy with current clients," or "I didn't receive any good leads." Alarm bells should now go off.

As their accountability partner, you must kindly and firmly indicate that the plan they created must be followed or they are failing on their commitments to the team, to you, and to their own success. You must be strong in this situation and not accept excuses. Regardless of their sales successes, regardless of their apparent business, and regardless of their stress, salespeople must be held accountable for living up to their action plan. They will thank you for it.

To help with this framework, access the Math of Success and Sales Action Plan Playbook in *The Happy Sales Manager Workbook* found at thehappysalesmanager.com.

KEY TAKEAWAYS

- Accountability is not micromanaging. It is providing a gentle reminder to each salesperson to do what will help them be successful.

- Setting clear expectations and getting agreement around those expectations from each salesperson are key to setting the groundwork for an effective culture of accountability.

- The Math of Success is an easy roadmap to establish ownership by each salesperson about their plan and execution.

- A regular cadence of one-to-one meetings is essential in providing the appropriate level of oversight.

- If you suffer from a need to be liked by your salespeople, realize that holding them accountable may be difficult for you and you will need to work hard in this area.

Improvement Exercise: How will you increase your level of accountability to ensure that everyone on your team is doing the "stuff" they are supposed to? Think about your team members and think about how each might react. How will you respond if individuals are negative about the accountability framework or if they push back? Take some time to plan how you will conduct these conversations.

Coaching

The second reason salespeople fail is that even though they are doing the right things, they aren't very good at them.

This is where coaching is needed. I could write an entire book on coaching since it is such a critical piece of the sales management puzzle and almost every sales manager I have encountered does not spend enough time doing it. Or if they do, they aren't doing it well. Telling a salesperson what to do is not coaching.

What is coaching?

Let's start with an agreed-upon understanding of what coaching is. It is the act of training, tutoring, and teaching others how to improve in the specific area of focus identified. Coaching *is not*:

- Doing it for them
- Rescuing them in a sales conversation
- Just telling them what to do
- Being their answer app so they don't have to learn and grow
- Allowing them to delegate up

Let's consider the different types of coaches that are most familiar to us.

- Sports coaches who run practice drills to help players improve in specific situations and review game or match performance with players to identify areas for improvement.
- Tutors or academic coaches who work with students to help them improve in certain subjects.

These examples can be applied to sales. As the manager, part of your mission is to help the people on your team improve and perform at a higher level.

As in any interaction with your team members, it is crucial that you have built trust and that they respect you. You can enhance this relationship by truly focusing on them and their growth in your coaching interactions. Remember, you must be team-focused as opposed to self-focused to be the most expert manager you can be. If you are not truly focused on the team and its growth and success, it will be hard to fake it. So get right with that first.

Opportunities abound to provide coaching, but you should not just rely on the informal, unplanned opportunities to coach.

Planned coaching

Planned coaching should occur in a regular cadence, preferably weekly. And you should have dedicated time for these coaching sessions. As part of this meeting, you should include a check-in on the accountability items, which were detailed in the previous chapter, such as their number of first discovery meetings and their activity commitments. If you approach this meeting as an opportunity to guide, tutor, and coach them to greater success, they will be more receptive than if you were to just look over their shoulder. As part of this meeting, you should conduct coaching. Plan to treat it like you would a sales conversation. You should be prepared to ask a lot of questions to understand how they are really doing and what they might need your help with. A recommended framework is:

- Complete the accountability portion of the meeting as described in the prior chapter.
- Discuss their highs and lows from the prior week. Be sure to focus on *why* those were their highs and lows. And be sure they are specific to them, not a collective team-high or -low. What are they proud of, and what do they wish they would have done better last week? It should not be focused on the bad economy or your high prices, etc.
- Ask them what skills or mindsets they are focused on improving this week and why. Always be asking them to improve and grow. Staying complacent just won't cut it in the fast-changing world in which we live.
- Debrief at least one sales call from the prior week. Feel free to use our Call Debriefing sheet which is found in *The Happy Sales Manager Workbook* at thehappysalesmanager.com. This sheet follows our prescribed sales process if you don't have your own sales process. Ask questions such as "What did they say when you asked [fill in the blank]?" Use the power of presumptive questioning to lead them to what they should be doing. If they aren't asking the right questions or following a repeatable sales process, this is a good place to course correct. If they are floundering and don't know where things stand with a particular opportunity, coach them to go back to the prospect and ask more

questions that uncover better information. There is no harm in them going back to a prospect and saying they were thinking about them and had some more questions.

- Pre-call plan any upcoming sales appointments with them. You may also use our Pre-call Planning sheet found in *The Happy Sales Manager Workbook* at thehappysalesmanager.com if you don't have your own format. Essentially, you should be helping them think about and plan for an upcoming conversation. Help them think about what they are going to say to build rapport, what they are going to say to ask about the financial considerations, how they are going to handle objections if faced, and what those objections might be, among other things. This is not purely a strategy conversation. This part of the conversation should also be focused on specifically what they are going to do and say.

- Conduct practice or mini role-play sessions with them to get them comfortable with what they will say in their upcoming sales appointments. Help them practice the "what ifs." Help them think through the questions they might be asked or the objections they might face. An easy way to approach this with the salesperson is just to say, "What are you going to say when the prospect says [fill in the blank]?"

- Provide observation and feedback. Remember your role is to continually challenge them to improve their skill set and their mindset. Provide some feedback when debriefing on how they handled a call and how they intend to approach an upcoming sales conversation. But refrain from just reverting to telling them what to do. You may want to lower their resistance first by saying something like, "Is it okay if I give you some feedback?" And then be sure to approach your feedback from the "I" perspective. Explain that something they said didn't hit right with *you*. And, again, refrain from just saying, "Say this . . . " Rather, ask them if they could have approached that part of the conversation differently. You could say, "How else could you say that?" or, "Is there a different way to approach that part of the conversation?" By doing this, they are the ones coming up with the solution. The more they are engaged in considering different and better approaches, the more they will grow and develop, and the less they will be reliant on you to direct them. This will free up your time, and they will become more confident and, ultimately, more successful.

Joint sales calls

In an ideal world, you would be regularly participating with each of your sales team members in joint sales calls, either on the phone, on Zoom/Teams, or in person. If you are conducting planned coaching sessions and helping them prepare for calls and debriefing calls as suggested, that is fantastic, but nothing beats watching a salesperson operate in a real live situation. Sometimes salespeople say all the right things when preparing with you for the call, but in the heat of the moment of a live sales situation, their stress heightens, their brain works less effectively, and they fail to perform in the same manner they had planned. This is normal. That is why practice is incredibly important, to help them elevate their confidence in the situation. But that practice doesn't replace witnessing for yourself how they operate in a live selling conversation. Therefore, you must participate in joint sales calls with your people purely for the coaching benefit.

Set the expectation that all your sellers must include you in a certain number of live sales conversations each week or month for coaching purposes. With newer, less experienced salespeople, you may require more joint calls, and with veterans, you may require fewer, but do not ignore those veterans. They can fall into bad habits, and they need to constantly sharpen their skills as well.

Meet with the salesperson in advance of the joint sales call to establish the agenda and who will be doing what. You need to participate in a limited or non-existent fashion on the sales call. Since the prospect may not know what your role is, it's perfectly okay to state that you routinely participate in sales conversations with the sales team to coach them. No harm in that.

Your main purpose is to observe and then provide feedback, which you should do in a debrief as quickly as possible following the conversation.

- Ask them how they think the conversation went.
- Ask them if they could have done something differently after looking back on it.
- Ask if you can provide feedback and then provide your feedback and observations. Provide your thoughts and feelings about how you reacted to what they said or did. And provide your thoughts on how the prospect was reacting to them.
- Gain commitment from them on what they will change or do differently in the future (if necessary).

You also have the opportunity to provide feedback and coaching on unplanned joint calls. Sometimes you need to jump onto a sales call as the manager. Although your title and authority are needed in these situations, be very clear that the salesperson is running the call. They must set the agenda, create a thorough pre-call plan, and indicate what they will do and what they want you to do and say. You are *not* there to take over. You are *not* there to show them how to do it. You are *not* there to be the hero. You will be playing a specific, defined, and limited role in the call. It is their prospect or client, their plan, and their victory when the business is secured. If a salesperson is relying on you to run the call, then you are restricting their ability to grow and develop. You are essentially holding them back and significantly restricting your ability to do your job to the best of your ability. If you are relied upon too heavily to win business for your salespeople, you are limiting the growth of the business. And, you must question why you need them if you are needed to close most or all of the business. But you may need to participate in a limited number of joint calls to help win business, which is fine; just remember to use it as a coaching opportunity: debrief the call and provide your feedback and observations by following the framework for coaching a joint call identified previously.

Unplanned coaching

Much of your coaching will likely occur on an ad hoc basis when a salesperson needs help with a certain situation or pops into your office to see if you have a minute to talk. Be careful that these don't turn into the help desk situation, where you become the "answer app" for all their sales situations, rather than allowing them to try and figure it out on their own before running it by you. These unplanned coaching moments may be the most opportune times to really help your salespeople grow, but you must be thoughtful since you may be in the habit of just answering their questions by telling them what to do. It is common to respond to a "What should I do in X situation" with the exact answer, but please refrain. The more you simply answer and send them on their way, the more frequently they will abdicate their role of using their brain and will increasingly ask you what to do. Instead, simply ask them what they are thinking about doing. And when they say, "I don't know. What do you think?" simply say, "What do you think I would tell you?" This way, you are engaging them in the solution. You are requiring them to use their brain to work it through, essentially helping them to build that muscle and restricting them from using you as their sales answer app—again.

This is super simple. But do not be fooled that it is easy. You will need to make a conscious effort to ask them to participate in the solution.

How much time to coach?

You may be concerned about the amount of time that I am suggesting you spend coaching—between the planned coaching meetings, the joint calls, and the unplanned coaching—but it *should* take much of your time. Nothing is more important than spending quality time with your salespeople and coaching them. According to research conducted by Objective Management Group, the most effective sales managers spend at least 50 percent of their time coaching their team members. This may seem daunting. If it does, commit to increasing your time coaching each person on your team. Set a specific amount of time to coach each one, and then do it. Then increase that number each month until you are coaching 50 percent of your time, if you're not already. This will take prioritizing coaching over other activities you may be distracted by. But the more you can coach your team, the better you will become at it, and the better they will be as salespeople, which means your team will more easily reach their sales goals.

KEY TAKEAWAYS

- Coaching is frequently misunderstood as directing, telling, or doing it for them to make their lives easier. Embrace that coaching is the act of helping others improve, not necessarily making it easier for them.

- Refuse to become the answer app for your salespeople. Cause them to think about how to solve their own problems.

- Include coaching as part of your regularly scheduled one-on-one sessions with the intent of ensuring they take responsibility for their growth and improvement as well.

- Do not take over a joint sales call. Rather plan those out in advance with the salesperson running the conversation.

Improvement Exercise: What is one item that you will change about the way you are coaching now?

Hiring and Onboarding

"Acquiring the right talent is the most important key to growth. Hiring was—and still is—the most important thing we do."

—Marc Benioff, Chair and CEO,
salesforce.com

Sales hiring is quite possibly the most difficult type of hiring to do and also the costliest. If you get it wrong, not only is sales growth negatively impacted, but also you will have added unnecessary costs, impacting profitability, not to mention the stress, frustration, and time that it costs you as the manager. Sales hiring requires a different approach than other positions, and if you haven't had much experience in hiring sales talent, you might be easily hoodwinked into hiring the wrong person for the position.

What to look for in sales candidates

Before you can hire the right candidate, you need to attract the right type of people to apply. If you are involved in writing the job description or maybe even directly participating in some of the recruiting, then ensure the description is very clear about what you're looking for and what they need to have accomplished.

Many hiring managers look for applicants who are outgoing or extroverted and are drawn to those who can connect with people and build relationships. Unfortunately, these aren't necessarily predictive of success in a sales position. It is not uncommon to look for talent that we feel most comfortable with or that is most similar to us. In general, hiring managers tend to focus on personality attributes that they'd like to get along with as opposed to traits and competencies that will reliably predict success in the sales position. This is a recipe for disaster.

Instead, you need to first pay attention to what you need the person to do to be successful. If you're hiring for inside sales, then obviously they need to be able to make their point on the phone as opposed to face to face. If it's an appointment setting position, like top of the funnel, they need to be rejection proof, good at building rapport very quickly, and able to be successful in a one-call close environment. Conversely, if you're hiring outside salespeople or individuals who need to conduct the full cycle of the sale, they need to conduct discovery conversations and qualify well also and, ultimately, gain the trust of the other party to follow their recommendations. That is very different from the skills needed for an appointment setter. My message is this: Just because they're in sales doesn't mean they're going to be successful in your sales role.

So make a checklist of the behaviors and attitudes that an individual must possess to be successful, not what their personality should be like but what they must do and the focus they must have to be successful. If you operate in a highly competitive market, then you need someone who can operate in a competitive environment. If it's very difficult to get to the decision maker, you need someone who has a proven track record of getting to the decision maker. If your typical sale cycle is long and complex with many people involved in the decision, you need someone that has that skill.

Also, be mindful that if you are hiring for a hunting role where the person needs to find their own opportunities and close them, that's very different than someone who is going to be given a book of business to expand. Just because they're in sales doesn't mean they can do both. Some people are better at one than the other and most don't possess both of those skill sets.

Next, make a list of what hasn't worked out in your environment. What we typically find is it's not the things that you know about as you're interviewing candidates that cause people to fail. It's the things that the sales manager glosses over, doesn't drill down on enough, and believes the person will be able to overcome. Be very honest about what's worked and what hasn't worked, and tailor your interviewing around those areas that have caused an issue in the past.

To help with this, think about people you have hired who didn't end up working out. Frequently this happened because you tried to hire the wrong person for the position. Yes, they're in sales and they assert that they can do the job that you need, but they aren't necessarily skilled or their background doesn't lend itself to predicting success in your role. Be very critical of what you missed that led to certain individuals failing on your sales team. Sadly, one of the most team-crushing outcomes of getting the sales hiring wrong is that sales managers tend to hang onto underperformers longer than they should because the job of hiring right is a distraction and a disruption.

Hiring managers often make mistakes in hiring people that

- Sold to very different decision-makers than your company does
- Worked for the name-brand company in their industry and your company is not

- Were the low-cost provider and you are not
- Had experience with expansion of existing accounts when you need a hunter
- Had shorter or much longer sale cycles in their previous roles
- Have only had transactional sales when you need to sell expensive, complex services
- Were part of a team that closed business, but didn't do it themselves

Lastly, in the job description, be very clear about what value your company brings to the potential candidate. Think of it like a marketing or sales description of what it is that your employees value about your company. Consider what the candidate will care about and construct a job description or job posting to speak to those ideal candidates and what matters to them. It is very similar to creating a value proposition for your sales efforts. If you could picture the ideal candidate, consider what they are going to care about.

With the list of skills needed for that specific job, the list of what hasn't worked out, and an idea of the value your company brings to the candidate, you should have a clear idea of who you are looking for. The job of hiring is hard because most hiring managers don't do it all that often so they are not that skilled at it, but it doesn't have to be a crapshoot. It starts with attracting the right people. So even if you have a well-staffed human resources and talent acquisition team, get involved in the job posting description so you can help characterize exactly what you're looking for. Frequently human resources professionals are uncomfortable in describing and creating the job posting that will attract the right candidates for sales positions.

Conducting effective interviews

Once you have found a pool of candidates, now comes the heavy lifting and filtering through these candidates to make sure that you select the appropriate individual. What I have noticed over the years is that sales managers who don't hire salespeople regularly may not be as comfortable conducting very thorough interviews with salespeople. They tend to project onto the salespeople those traits that they need the salesperson to possess during the interview. It's also human nature to like certain people who seem similar to us. But relying on your instinct to make sales hiring decisions can get you into trouble. First, you aren't doing it on a regular enough basis so you won't be an expert at it. Second, salespeople might be better at interviewing than you are because they're in sales and that is what they should be doing with prospects. One of the biggest tricks that candidates employ is asking many questions that get the hiring manager talking. And because the hiring manager got to talk a lot, they end up liking the candidate. It is a weird psychology that causes this to happen. Therefore, try to refrain from answering questions until you have developed your opinion about whether they can effectively do the job you need them to do. Simply indicate you don't have a lot of time and you would like to cover some other items first, but you will eventually get to their questions.

Be sure to conduct your interviews in a robust fashion. Don't rush through them. Really focus on what the person might be missing and what might be a hurdle for them rather than just the good stuff. If you do this, then you don't need to conduct a lot of interviews with each individual candidate. You don't need to conduct numerous interviews to determine whether they're going to be a fit or not.

I've witnessed over the years hiring managers glossing over candidates' weaknesses. I've done this myself. If they are great but lack skills in one necessary area, you might gloss over that gap. I can't tell you how many times hiring managers have conducted interviews and then shared that they just are uncomfortable about an area, or they're not sure about something else. If you are thinking it, you have to ask about it and you have to get them to defend it. It's their job to explain to you why they are appropriate for the position. Don't project onto them that they can do the job if they're missing certain elements. Don't assume that they can pick skills and requirements up easily if some are missing from their experience.

If you can keep your subjective opinions about a candidate out of the equation until later in the interviewing process, you will have more success. The best way to do that is to use a predictive assessment specifically for sales early in the recruiting process before you even interview them. I happen to be a huge fan of the Objective Management Group's sales-specific assessments, mainly because they are not personality based or adapted from a social setting; rather, they are predictive of an individual being successful in a specific sales position. You may access a free trial if interested by going to thehappysalesmanager.com. Using a tool such as this early in the interviewing process, before you've even interviewed them, provides you with a completely objective analysis of an individual, which will help you tailor your questions to their gaps. It's super easy to identify a candidate's strengths in a sales interview, but it's not that easy to identify their gaps. As I said before, the gaps or the weaknesses are the things that typically cause a salesperson to be unsuccessful in a particular sales role.

A great book on interviewing is *Who* by Geoff Smart. It's a short read, and it's not specifically about sales interviewing; however, it's a good guide for interviewing in general.

In addition to the standard practice of creating a list of questions that you're going to ask every candidate, I would suggest you categorize the interview process into three different groups as follows:

1. General questions you will ask every candidate
2. Specific questions related to this candidate and their resume
3. A sales simulation

Let's look at each one of these individually.

General questions. General questions are those that you're going to ask every candidate, such as:

- "Why are you looking for a new position?"
- "What was appealing about the ad that caused you to apply for this position?"
- "Please give me some information about your success in sales. Why do you think you are better than other candidates?"

These types of questions will provide a laundry list that you can pull from for all your interviews. You can also find a more comprehensive list in *The Happy Sales Manager Workbook,* found at thehappysalesmanager.com.

Specific questions related to this candidate. In preparation for the interview, you should have spent some time with their resume and maybe their LinkedIn profile and circled some things that you want to ask about. It's not unusual for a salesperson to tout their successes and how great they were. So start with what they presented and dig a little deeper about what is in their resume and on their LinkedIn profile. Do not be bashful about asking questions about their resume and going deep in terms of what made them successful. For instance, if someone says they were the number one salesperson in three of the last four years, ask them what happened to the one year that they weren't. Also, ask them what they mean by "they were the number one salesperson." After all, that could mean one out of two or it could mean they are one out of 100, which is quite different. I would then also ask for more specifics around that. For instance, how much of that business came from existing customers versus new customers? Were these new accounts all sold exclusively by the candidate, or did they participate in a team-selling environment? What you're trying to uncover in these types of questions is how their history relates to the position that you're interviewing them for. Don't just assume that because they did things successfully that those experiences will necessarily convert to what they need to do to be successful in your specific position.

Be certain to put your skeptic's hat on. Do not take anything they say at face value. Dig deeper. If you need to be liked, this may be difficult, but hiring the wrong salesperson will make your life so much harder.

If you think they may be lacking a certain skill, ask them about it. Simply indicate that you aren't quite comfortable with a certain aspect and tell them you need them to convince you of how you are going to get over that particular concern. Remember, you're hiring for a sales position, so if they can't "convince" you of their worth for the position, then what makes you think that they'll be able to get prospective buyers to buy from them?

Sales simulation. Finally, conduct a sales simulation with the candidate. Don't do the stupid "sell me this pencil" trick. Instead, ask them to conduct a sales conversation with you as if you are a potential buyer for their current sales role. They will be familiar with what they're going to try and sell you and how they're going to conduct the sales conversation. This way you can see how they actually operate rather than during a completely made-up scenario. I would suggest that you have some type of scorecard created for this simulation, so if certain elements don't make sense, you can score this individual against those. If you're having them do a first discovery call, maybe you want to observe if they follow a sales process or if they just ramble. Their sales process doesn't have to be identical to what your team follows, but it will be enlightening to see if they follow one; then if you ask questions about it after the simulation, you may learn more about how they operate. In this simulation, don't necessarily be the easiest prospect but also don't be the biggest jerk in the world either. Just allow the person to conduct the sales conversation. Pay attention to their level of talking and telling. Are they accomplished at asking questions and probing without making you feel icky? When conducting the sales simulation, be prepared to ask questions and provide some objections or some pushback. This might feel uncomfortable for you to conduct a role-play, but how can you tell if they can sell if you don't get the opportunity to see them try it?

After the interview, simply say, "We'll be in touch with the next steps after we complete interviews with other candidates." Make a note if any candidate doesn't just take this, rather wants to know if there is any reason why they wouldn't move to the next step. This is a great sign, but few will likely ask. Be prepared to answer though. Those that do ask, will be better not taking brush offs in their selling situations too.

Assign a project. If you like the candidate and you are anticipating moving to the next step with them, then give them a project next. I would suggest that you only do this with a handful of candidates that are your final candidates.

The most logical project to give them would be to ask them to put together a 90-day plan of how they're going to get up to speed and produce results as quickly as possible. It's not going to be perfect, but it's going to show you that they're willing to put the effort in to think about the position and put some work in to try to understand what they need to do to be successful in the position. It will also show you their ability to think sequentially, as in, are they able to go from point *A* to point *B* to Point *C*? If you give them a week to complete that project and they don't deliver it to you in a week, that's a very bad sign.

Interviewing inexperienced salespeople

If your role calls for you to hire people who don't have sales experience, then obviously you can't do some of the things that you can do with experienced salespeople. They're not going to have a sales history. They're not going to be able to conduct a sales simulation.

So instead, discuss the following:

- Situations where they've overcome adversity and stuck with something even though it was hard (Since many candidates are prepared to share something that they've had to overcome, ask them to share one, then another, then another. Dive deeper to get something more than a prepared answer.)
- Their failures and what caused them to go in a different direction
- Why they think they would be successful in any given sales role if they haven't had sales experience before
- What type of rejection they have faced in their life and when they have been denied something (Maybe they

tried out for a sports team that they didn't make or the lead in a school play? Learn what they did when those situations occurred. You are trying to uncover how they handle rejection because, as you know, rejection is a constant part of sales.)

And if they have never had to overcome any difficulty, adversity, or rejection, then you may want to proceed very cautiously. When hiring for a beginner sales role, the most important skills to consider are their grit and determination. Will they fight through when the going gets tough? If they have always lived on easy street, you have no way of knowing.

Bonus interviewing tips

- Do not linger and elongate the interviewing process if you have some good candidates. Candidates are like bananas: if they are left on the shelf, they will rot. They will go get other positions if you do not engage with them quickly. Get back to them and keep them engaged.
- Use a scorecard for all of your interviews. And if you're just not sure about an individual, call them and ask them to explain themselves, or ask them to share with you why you shouldn't be worried about a particular situation.
- You may want to conduct joint interviews. Maybe have someone else participate in the interview with you to experience the candidate differently than you do. I would suggest having someone who is not similar to you from a personality or style standpoint. If your salespeople sell to financial individuals, ask your CFO to sit in or listen to a recording. If you have someone

similar to the targeted decision maker in your sales team, have them sit in or listen to the recording.

- Be open to salespeople from other industries. Too frequently I have seen managers suffer because they chose to hire the person that knew the industry as opposed to the best salesperson. Even if a candidate comes from your industry, they need the ability to sell your products and services under your company's culture. Just because they know the industry does not mean they will be successful selling for you. It is easier to teach a great salesperson about your products and services than it is to teach an industry expert to become a great salesperson.
- Take calls from salespeople. Have all sales calls come to you, and if one of them is good, invite them to have a longer conversation. Witness them trying to sell you something, then turn it around. Compliment them and ask if they would have any interest in talking about a position with your company.

Onboarding

Once you've hired your salesperson, you can now *start* the onboarding process. However, now is not the first time to *think* about your onboarding process. You should do that before hiring someone.

Onboarding needs just as much attention as the interviewing and hiring process. The goal of onboarding is to get the new hire up to speed as quickly as possible so they can start producing a return on investment as quickly as feasible. Plus, a good salesperson wants to be out selling as quickly as possible. Keep this goal in mind as you onboard salespeople. If they just aren't cutting it and not doing what you need them to do, get rid of them as quickly as possible. Cut your losses early.

The length of your onboarding will depend on the complexity of what the new hire needs to learn. Most of our clients say a three- to six-month time period is appropriate, but yours may differ. The keys to successful and speedy onboarding are:

- Set expectations every step of the way
- Be engaged with them, but don't have them attached to your hip
- Realize there are no "plug and play" candidates (meaning they need guidance)

Let's assume that your onboarding plan is a 90-day plan. In that case, break down your expectations in the following increments:

- Day 1
- Week 1
- Month 1
- Month 2
- Month 3

For each increment, set expectations for what they need to have accomplished, what they are responsible for, and what set activities they should be engaging in. You may have new hires involved in selling activities in the first week, or you may not have them focused on selling activities until later in their onboarding. Regardless, whenever they are expected to conduct selling activities, make sure they are doing them.

Equip them with knowledge. For them to be successful, you need to equip them with the necessary knowledge. I am not talking about technical knowledge. They need that too, but I am not an expert on the technical requirements of your sales roles. In this case, I am focusing on the necessary knowledge and tools to conduct successful sales conversations, including:

- A large list of the best, most thought-provoking questions that will help them uncover the true needs or problems of the prospect
- Stories of solutions you have provided for clients that they can use when describing what your company does
- The advantages of using your services compared to other options the prospects have
- An understanding of how to calculate the ROI of your products or services from the client's perspective
- The Math of Success necessary for this position, meaning how many first appointments they need each week to generate enough opportunities based on their typical closing ratios, and the likely level and type of activity that will be necessary to generate those appointments
- Clear, understandable expectations at every step
- Regular standing check-ins on their progress

Spend significant time focused on these elements, and assuming you selected the right person for the position, the new hire will have greater success more quickly.

New hire's responsibilities. As you teach them, make sure you aren't spoon-feeding them. The idea behind setting expectations is to make them aware that you and your team will provide support, but it's their job to get what they need to be successful in their role. To that end, you may ask other team members to share certain elements with them. Put those team members on notice, but it should be the new hire's responsibility to reach out and schedule time with team members. You do not have to be the master scheduler of everything. Give the new hire the chance to reach out and schedule for themselves. By doing this, you allow the new hire and the other team members to connect differently than if you were to do everything. Just set clear expectations about what needs to be accomplished and by when, then empower the individual by letting them manage their own schedule.

Don't offload new hires. Avoid offloading the new hire onto one of your sales superstars. I know this might sound like a great idea, but frequently, your better salespeople have been so successful for a while that they may cut corners. So they may not be the shining example of what you want the new hire to learn. However, if someone on the sales team is an aspiring manager or team leader, they could be a good fit for helping to get the new hire up to speed. But you still need to be engaged, checking in and making sure that the new hire is progressing as expected. Do not abdicate your role to others.

Remember that the quicker you can get the new hire up to speed and fully producing the better for everyone, but do not cut corners with their onboarding.

Feel free to access our 90-day onboarding checklist found in *The Happy Sales Manager Workbook* at thehappysalesmanager.com.

KEY TAKEAWAYS

- Be precise in determining what skills and mindset are necessary for success in any sales role you are hiring for and help HR articulate these in the job posting.

- Be critical of yourself and the circumstances as to why certain salespeople did not work out.

- Take your time to prepare and use checklists to ensure you approach each sales interview with a clear goal in mind of what is needed for success, and to avoid not asking the difficult questions because you need to be liked.

- Refrain from liking a candidate too much and glossing over areas where they might be deficient.

- Read the book *Who* by Geoff Smart and apply its interviewing principles.

- Plan the onboarding process in advance of hiring the individual.

- Create precise expectations for every stage of a new hire's onboarding.

- Stay closely engaged with the new hire but enlist others to help get the person ramped up as quickly as possible.

Improvement Exercise: Create a list of the specific items necessary for success in your various sales roles. Focus on the activities and behaviors they need to execute for success. Then make a list of the reasons others have failed. Finally create a list of questions to use in interviewing that will enable you to more easily uncover the gaps that may hinder success.

Tactical Elements
of Your Role

In this section, we will address some of the tactical items related to sales management that you will need to consider:

- Sales Organization Structure
- Compensation Plans
- Pipeline Management
- Conducting Inspiring Sales Meetings
- Sales Process

Sales Organization Structure

A ROUND PEG DOES NOT FIT INTO A SQUARE HOLE

Just like how different people in the various disciplines of business have different skills and thus, are most appropriate for different roles, salespeople also have different skills.

There isn't a one-size-fits-all approach to the structure of your sales organization. All businesses have nuances that suggest a customized structure for the needs of the business. But frequently people ask me about the "right" structure. Most companies' sales structure is built around the people on their team, as opposed to from the ground up, in a manner that is most effective and efficient. The core principles of who you should have in the roles on your sales team apply to both situations, though.

Salespeople do not come in one variety, so you need salespeople on your team with different core skill sets to maximize sales and profit growth. So regardless of the industry you are in or the size of your business, don't get caught up in thinking that some other company's sales team structure is superior. Focus on what is needed for your market, what your unique company attributes are, and what the mission is. If you start with the goal in mind—and the behaviors necessary to reach that goal—you will have great success in constructing your department in the right way.

When I first started Braveheart, we were on the heels of the Great Recession in 2009, but we were successful right away since so many company owners were frustrated by the lack of prospecting that their sales teams were undertaking. They had learned the hard way that they didn't have hunters on their team; instead, they had account managers who were great at fielding requests for additional products or services from their existing book of accounts, essentially glorified order takers. Some can adapt and learn how to be more effective hunters, and some are going to struggle, so it won't be worth the ROI to try and train them to become hunters.

Difference between hunters and account managers

Far more salespeople are successful account managers than true hunters. The skills and mindset required to be a great hunter are somewhat different than account managers.

Hunters' skills:

- Expert at qualifying
- Effective at reaching decision-makers
- Aren't sidelined by rejection

- Ability to sell their and their company's value while being consultative in their approach
- Ability to not worry about what the prospect is thinking of them

In an account management role, the salesperson may be able to get away with not possessing any of these competencies. Those skills would be helpful but likely not necessary. An account manager needs to have the mindset to manage and immerse themselves over time in their client's business. Sure some salespeople out there are adept at both these roles and possess a high level of effectiveness at both, but those individuals are rare.

Unfortunately, unwitting leaders can create an environment that causes individuals to become account managers, as they reward the attributes of an account manager by taking perfectly good hunters and having them manage their clients after the business is won. Conversely, managers sometimes try to have their account managers be hunters. An obvious indicator that you have an account manager who is not well-suited to hunting, even if they are supposed to hunt for new accounts, is that they fill their time tending to existing accounts. They never seem to have adequate time to get to the required hunting and share many excuses as to why they cannot find the time to hunt. So, if you have this situation on your hands and you need more new clients, you may be better off hiring true hunters rather than trying to convert account managers to hunters, or change a zebra's stripes as it were.

My advice is to let hunters hunt and have account managers manage accounts.

Hunters love the chase. They want to go out and find new business. They enjoy learning about new prospects and their businesses. They probably don't like the ongoing relationships that they must build to effectively manage ongoing accounts. Conversely, account managers enjoy ongoing relationships. They don't enjoy the hunt for new accounts and when asked to do more hunting, may stress out.

Appointment setters vs full-cycle salespeople

Many organizations have discovered that they can organize their sales team along different lines. They may be able to find lower-paid inside salespeople or appointment setters that can make many more contacts with prospects than full-cycle salespeople (your hunters and account managers) tend to. This then frees up their full-cycle salespeople to focus on closing the business. If you have or are considering a structure where you have some appointment setters and some full-cycle salespeople, be certain to set clear expectations for the different roles.

Appointment setters should have a target number of appointments to make per week, and they must be *qualified* appointments, meaning that the appointments they set must meet certain qualifications.

And then if this is adhered to, full-cycle salespeople must be expected to close a certain percentage of those qualified opportunities. Additionally, as the title would imply, full-cycle salespeople could (and maybe should) be expected to also find their own opportunities beyond what the appointment setter lines up for them. This structure tends to also create expectations that appointment setters can be promoted into full-cycle salespeople. This can work great, but you must understand the significant differences between the two roles.

Appointment setter role. This role requires a relentless focus on the volume of outreach. It is not unusual for this role to necessitate 60 or more phone calls per day, along with email follow-ups. It might be tempting to just unleash an untrained, inexperienced individual to do this role, but don't do that. Don't just throw a newbie to the wolves and let them figure it out. Sure, you might not be paying them as much as you do your full-cycle salespeople, but if they are not trained and coached to perform up to an expected level of effectiveness, you will not only be wasting money on them, but you also may be damaging your company's reputation with the targets that they are focused on. These individuals need to be able to:

- Quickly develop rapport
- Hunt
- Engage in one-call closes (closing for an appointment)
- Find prospects consistently
- Get commitments
- Handle rejection
- Be coachable
- Have intrinsic motivation (because the role can be thankless)
- Stay in the moment
- Not need approval
- Qualify

If you have or are going to embark on a structure where you have appointment setters, you need to be clear that they may have the opportunity to advance into full-cycle sales but that different skills and mindsets are necessary to be effective in full-cycle sales.

Full-cycle sales role. As stated previously, full-cycle salespeople need to possess different competencies than appointment setters to be successful. Not only do they need to stay in the moment, have no need for approval, and have the qualifying competency, but they also have an additional list of competencies that are required for success including:

- Taking responsibility for outcomes
- Following the sales process
- Gaining trust
- Using consultative sales skills
- Selling value
- Ability to "connect the dots"
- Feeling comfortable discussing money
- Negotiating
- Exercising the appropriate amount of patience
- Closing

Customer experience teams with a sales focus

You may also want to consider what level of account manager your customers truly need. Are there customer-experience or customer-service individuals who can adequately handle the bulk of the relationship after the business is won? You may want to consider this if you are maximizing their positive impact on the customer relationship. Frequently, companies have individuals who hunt and close the business and are either also managing the relationship ongoing or handing it off to an account manager, but the customer experience team has most of the interaction with the customer on an ongoing basis. Some companies bring on account managers to fill in the gap between customer experience and sales. If your salespeople need to be out selling more and your customer experience team is not operating in a sales capacity, you may want to consider an alternative approach. Could the customer experience team be trained to ask better questions, be slightly more inquisitive, and be a little bit more proactive rather than just being purely service-oriented?

My company, Braveheart Sales, has helped many companies tweak the expectations of the customer experience (customer service, project manager) teams to include some "sales" focus. They may not have sales quotas, but they can certainly have expectations around the types of questions they will ask and the type of interaction they will have with customers. After all, selling is just excellent communication with the intent of identifying what the other party needs in order to accomplish their goals. So consider equipping the customer experience team with improved communication and questioning skills to enable them to uncover potential opportunities where your company can help the customer more. Don't try to turn them into full-blown salespeople unless they have the capacity and desire to be so, but having them be a little more inquisitive can pay huge dividends both for the company and the customer.

KEY TAKEAWAYS

- Salespeople do not come in a one-size-fits-all variety, and you may need to consider different roles for different needs.

- Just because an individual was successful in an appointment setter role does not guarantee they will succeed in a full-cycle sales role.

- Typically salespeople don't naturally excel at both hunting and account management. Be careful not to turn hunters into account managers and vice versa.

- Sometimes customer experience or customer service personnel can take on a greater role in account management.

Improvement Exercise: Dream of your ideal sales organization and define the behaviors necessary for the different functions within that organizational structure. Identify the roles that you need to be performed as opposed to the people that fill those roles now. Next, identify the gaps in your current organization. Can people be trained in certain skills, or do people need to be moved to other positions where they can have more success?

Compensation Plans

"Money is only one form of compensation."

—Frank Sonnenberg, The Path to a Meaningful Life

There are too many compensation plan structures, so we won't attempt to address them all; however, I do want to give you some options to consider and some elements of structuring a plan.

Structuring a plan to reward desired behaviors and outcomes

What behavior to reward? Frequently, compensation plans reward the type of behavior that they've always rewarded, but the owner of the company or the leader of the sales team is frustrated because they really want the salespeople to do something different. Unfortunately, the salespeople don't do it because the compensation plan doesn't reward them to do it. For instance, if you want more appointments, then figure out some kind of component of the compensation plan that will reward your salespeople for securing more appointments.

If you want them to sell more of a particular type of service or business or product, then reward that focus. Zero in on what you want, then make the compensation plan reward that.

Don't rely solely on the plan. You have to understand that the compensation plan alone is not going to drive the right behaviors. You might be thinking that I'm being contradictory to what I said before, which is to reward the right behaviors. But the reality is that some, if not many, people on your sales team are not going to be motivated solely by the commission or extra compensation they can make by closing more business. Remember that different people are motivated differently, and the majority of salespeople are actually not completely money-motivated. You have to consider this. Regardless of the compensation plan structure, it is still your job to manage behaviors, not just let the plan manage the behaviors for you.

Team composition and what you expect them to do. In the previous chapter, I shared the difference between account managers and hunters and full-cycle salespeople and appointment setters. And in section 1, I discussed the fact that different people are motivated differently. You must consider these things. For instance, you want different behaviors out of account managers than you do hunters, so consider customizing the plan for the different behaviors necessary for the different roles.

Think about what you're trying to accomplish with the plan and let that guide the components of the plan. For instance, if you have pure hunters, then they need to be compensated based on their success in bringing in new accounts. Getting a prospect to be interested in your business to the point that they're willing to sit down and talk about it and maybe buy your services or your products is harder than expanding relationships with existing accounts that already know and appreciate your company. Therefore, I am a proponent of compensating hunters more for the hard work that they do to get new clients. I would suggest a larger upside potential in their pay due to variable compensation than account managers. Additionally, truly excellent hunters tend to be more money-motivated than others, so you may want to have a lower-base salary with a larger commission structure for hunters, which would be enticing to those individuals and would have more impact on shaping their behavior. If you have salespeople who must do both hunting for new business and managing existing accounts, then you may need to consider how you want them to spend their time. You don't want them to ignore their new business-generating activities, and you also don't want them to ignore their existing customers. The compensation plan should factor in that time. So if you want them to focus 50 percent of their time on hunting for new business and 50 percent of their time tending to existing accounts in a service capacity, then you may need a hybrid plan.

Account managers are critically important to maintaining your business. Without them focusing on the existing clients, your team will have to hunt and hunt and hunt. So they need to be appropriately compensated for that, but you may not even need or want to compensate them with variable compensation. You could just pay them a straight salary to take great care of the customers. Of course, if part of their job is to expand the business with your existing customers, whether you pay them a commission to do so or not, you need to give them very clear expectations about what their goals are in this regard. Then with those clear expectations, you could offer a commission, but remember to pay attention to how they are motivated. Many account managers are not motivated by money or any external reward. They are motivated by taking great care of the client and by doing what is right for the customer.

If a base salary plus commission is the right structure for your account managers, then ensure that account managers are paid a larger portion of their compensation with their base salary. This is the opposite of what I suggest for hunters.

It is possible to compensate salespeople based on their new business production as well as their success managing existing accounts. You could easily have a component that pays out based on closed business, then either employ the carrot or the stick approach associated with their account servicing duties. If your culture is a "carrot" culture, then provide a component in the plan for extra commission if the individual completes a certain number of client account reviews where specific elements are discussed. If, on the other hand, your culture is more of a "stick," you could have a component for servicing accounts, but characterize it as a requirement to receive their full commission.

Don't constantly restructure. If you have a compensation plan in place that pays some form of variable compensation for the production of business, be careful with changing it. It's more difficult to restructure a program than it is to start one from scratch because there's always this natural tendency for the salespeople to get concerned or upset that you're trying to do something to them or you are intentionally trying to restrict their pay. And, frankly, they have a reason for concern. One of the biggest concerns that salespeople voice is their unhappiness with an ever-changing sales commission plan. And, certainly, plenty of companies out there change their commission plans because they think that salespeople are not deserving of the compensation. Typically, this is because the plan was not well thought-out to start or because the leaders are relying on the compensation plan to be the fix for everything.

Keep it simple. The simpler the plan is to communicate and understand, the better. If you can make it easy for them to understand how they're going to get rewarded, you'll have better success than something that is highly complex and maybe captures every little thing.

The simple math

I want you to consider what's going to be right for you from a math perspective. As we have established, you will have your own unique plan. Consider your:

- Profit margins
- Size of transactions
- Types of salespeople
- Market
- Elements of selling

You will need to consider all these things and apply them to construct the right plan for your business. There is not a single most effective compensation plan for all circumstances. But if you remember the first two key elements—reward the behavior you want and realize that the compensation plan alone will not cause people to change and do exactly what you want them to do—you can then start to structure your plan.

As you structure it, you can use some simple math to guide you. If you think about salespeople similarly to how you would a piece of equipment in a manufacturing plant, this may make it easier to consider the financial components. If you were going to buy a new piece of equipment, you would do some type of ROI analysis. You would calculate how many more widgets you needed to produce over what period of time to justify spending money on the new piece of equipment. You should think about salespeople the same way. You have to take into consideration what you're paying them and the production that is required to produce an appropriate ROI.

1. Consider their base salary if there is one, and what their projected total compensation would be if they

meet the sales expectations. In other words, if they're doing what you want them to do and generating sales to meet their quota, how much would they or should they earn in total compensation, including the variable portion of their compensation and their base salary?

2. What is an appropriate ROI for that particular salesperson? No, you don't want a different compensation plan for each salesperson, but you do want one for your different types of salespeople, as mentioned earlier. Consider how much you have invested in the salesperson. In other words, how much will you pay them to do their job? A typical rule of thumb is they should be generating somewhere between three times and five times their annual compensation in gross profit for your company, depending on whether you are in a high-gross-margin business or a low-gross-margin business. Remember, you want an adequate return on investment based on what you are investing in the salesperson, so that's a starting place for this calculation. Don't be shy about expecting higher-paid salespeople to produce more business. If you maintain the ratio of three times to five times their total compensation, that will guide you to the sales goals appropriate for different levels of base salary.

Base Salary + Commission on Their Sales Made = Total Compensation

Gross Profit of Sales Made = 3x to 5x Their Total Compensation

Example:
Salesperson's base salary is $75,000 and sales goal is $750,000 @ 75% Gross Margin (Gross Profit is $562,500)

- For 3x ROI: $562,500 divided by 3 = $187,500. Since their base salary is $75,000, the commission plan could pay $112,500.

- For 5x ROI: $562,500 divided by 5 = $112,500. Base salary is $75,000, so the commission plan could pay $37,500.

Contests and campaigns

Add-on situations like campaigns and contests should not be standard operating procedures replacing the overall compensation plan. If you always need to have a campaign or contest to drive behaviors around a specific thing, step back, take a bigger view of your compensation plan, and determine what is missing from the established goals or the coaching and feedback around their performance. Contests and campaigns are great for sprints, as they are short-lived and targeted to a specific thing you want them to do, whereas the overall compensation plan is designed for the marathon. So just keep in mind that contests and campaigns should not be something that just goes on and on and on. Otherwise, they become part of the compensation plan or an entitlement.

When you do run a contest, **ask the individual salespeople what they want for their reward**. Set the dollar amount associated with the reward, but then give each person a choice of how they want to be rewarded. This will be far more impactful than your selecting one specific award regardless of who wins. For example, some people think a trip is a great reward and others do not. It is possible that going on a trip is a huge ordeal for some people, especially those who have young children. It isn't a great reward for everyone. If possible, provide a selection of rewards that are roughly the same dollar amount, then each individual can select what will be most motivating to them. And refrain from just providing a cash reward, to ensure it is viewed as different from the normal compensation plan.

Also ensure that **everybody can win**, meaning that every individual that reaches a specific goal of the campaign will get rewarded. Do not construct a contest with just one or a couple of winners. It does no good to run a three-month campaign or a month-long program if it's clear who the one winner will be in the first couple of weeks. This won't inspire the rest of the team to hustle through the length of the contest. Construct a plan where anyone who reaches the threshold receives an award. But, remember, the campaign alone won't necessarily cause people to operate differently. It will take constant communication and coaching to keep it front and center for everyone on the team.

KEY TAKEAWAYS

- Structure a compensation plan that is right for your team, and consider a plan that is different for hunters versus account managers and all the various roles.

- Keep the plan as simple as possible.

- Your compensation plan should reward the behavior you want.

- The plan alone will not fix behavior issues; your management and guidance are required regardless of the plan.

- Target between 3x and 5x ROI when the salesperson is meeting their sales goals.

- Take care to fully model and explain any changes to an existing plan, as salespeople often fear the worst when a plan is changed.

- Use contests and campaigns as appropriate for short-term motivation and focus.

- Be very clear that the plan is only the plan for this year and that due to market and company changes, it may need to be tweaked in the future.

Improvement Exercise: Ask yourself if the plan as it exists today rewards the behaviors you want. If not, how might you change it to reinforce the behaviors you want while maintaining an adequate ROI related to your salespeople?

Pipeline Management

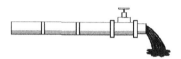

The sales pipeline should have velocity and flow like an oil pipeline. Otherwise, the pipeline becomes a pipe dream.

I have seen managers spend far too much time focused on the pipeline in sales meetings. It is common practice to painstakingly go through each opportunity in public only to hear the same old names on the list without any significant movement. So it's important to build a more predictive pipeline.

Pipeline structure and key components

A pipeline has two main purposes: to reliability predict what will close for planning, financial, and resource reasons and to focus attention on the necessary items that actually close more business.

Too frequently the pipeline is just a repository of "stuff" or opportunities that a salesperson hopes will lead to a close. Well, as the old saying goes, "Hope is not a strategy." The pipeline should bucket opportunities based on what you know about the situation and what will create a higher likelihood of closing.

With that said, I can't just outline one specific magical pipeline structure that will effortlessly enable salespeople to close more business. Just like your company, products and services, and target customers are unique, so, too, is your pipeline. So I can help you with the structure, but I can't say exactly what should go in it.

As you create the structure, focus on making your pipeline reliably predictive. In an ideal world, your weighted pipeline—the percentages applied to each opportunity in each stage of the pipeline—would accurately project the revenue that occurs. In my experience, this is rarely true unless one spends a massive amount of time unpacking the opportunities in the pipeline by going through opportunity by opportunity and evaluating which will close when rather than letting the pipeline do the work for them.

The wrong way to structure a pipeline

Not focusing on the likelihood of closing. Too often pipelines are characterized by what happened, not the likelihood of opportunities closing. For instance, it is not uncommon for a pipeline to have a stage indicating a meeting was held. Later in this same pipeline include a stage indicating a proposal was sent. It might look something like this:

1. Lead/Target
2. 1st Meeting
3. Demo/Sample
4. Proposal
5. Negotiation
6. Close

The flaw here is assuming that just because something took place, the opportunity is more likely to close. This is not necessarily true. Too often we create the false hope that if a salesperson goes through these stages, they will miraculously have more business than they can stand. With this pipeline, they are more focused on getting "stuff" into the pipeline and keeping it there rather than focusing on the precision of the questioning during qualifying, with a level of skepticism about the viability of an opportunity. You need them to be qualifying opportunities, not adding stuff to the pipeline. When qualifying opportunities, I suggest they actually shift the focus to *disqualifying* opportunities unless the opportunities meet certain criteria. A full, or what I call fluffy, pipeline is not productive. It creates a false sense of security and reduces the angst that a salesperson might have to urgently generate more business. This is dangerous.

So, again, the focus shouldn't be on making sure a step in the pipeline happens but rather on closing the opportunity. As another example, I often see salespeople push to get a demo or to send a sample, and then rapidly produce a proposal, believing the proposal itself will close the business. Sadly, when the structure is focused on these checklist stages, such as "conduct demo" or "send sample" and then "produce a proposal," salespeople tend to be less efficient than they otherwise could be. It is not uncommon to hear that the team closed only 25 or 15 percent of the proposals they put out. That is a lot of wasted energy, and potentially wasted resources as well if others need to be involved in producing the proposals. Just checking the box on the stages in this type of pipeline produces inconsistent and unsatisfactory results.

Includes negotiations. If the salesperson has done a great job of asking questions, qualifying, and producing a proposal that documents the agreement, then why should there be negotiation? Okay, I understand some negotiations may happen, but why assume that the prospect will do so? Making this assumption is just bad mojo. A better practice would be to not produce a proposal unless the opportunity is fully qualified and the prospect is on board. Realistically, the proposal should be the documentation of the details previously discussed. It should not be a document produced to begin negotiations.

A better way to structure the pipeline

To create a predictive pipeline, start with what you need to know to cause an opportunity to have a higher likelihood of closing. Each business likely has certain triggers or tipping points that indicate a higher likelihood of success. The pipeline should be structured so it reinforces the sales process and what questions need to be answered to move an opportunity along. The sales process and pipeline structure are closely linked. The more you know about a particular opportunity (by following a repeatable sales process) and the more intimate the salesperson becomes with the prospect, the more one should be able to predict closing success and, therefore, the further along in the pipeline the opportunity should sit.

A better pipeline structure could be something like this:

1.   Knowing why lead/target is willing to engage in a first discovery meeting
2.   Understanding how compelling their need or problem is
3.   Determining whether you can produce an adequate ROI for them from their perspective
4.   Understanding the decision-making process (all facets—who, how, why, etc.)
5.   Creating the proposal (summary of what was previously discussed and agreed to)
6.   Closing

In this scenario, one would not produce a proposal unless they have a high degree of certainty that the opportunity will close. The proposal is merely a documentation of what has already been discussed. Once the proposal is produced, there should be a 75 percent or higher closing ratio. It should be a rare occurrence that the opportunity does not close. Think about the efficiency associated with this mentality of focusing more on fully qualifying the opportunities before doing the busy work of producing a proposal.

This structure requires more thoughtful consideration of what it takes for an opportunity to move from one stage to the next. It requires salespeople to adhere to a discipline around asking the right questions to uncover how likely the opportunity is to close and also confronting the real possibility that an opportunity is not a good fit.

Effective Pipeline Staging

Stage	Stage One	Stage Two	Stage Three	Stage Four	Stage Five	Stage Six
What	Target Willing to Meet	How Compelling?	ROI for Client	Decision Making	Proposal Ready	Close
Sample Questions	What causes you to want to meet?	How important is it to resolve this situation? Why is it important now?	What is the cost of not fixing this? If I told you the solution would cost between $x, and $y what would you say?	Who else do you include when you make decisions like this? What would cause you to not fix this?	If I get you the proposal by Tues, can we meet at 10:00 on Wed to discuss?	When do you want to get started fixing your problem?

Don't focus on the timeline for each stage. I am not going to tell you exactly what length of time an opportunity should or will stay in each stage of the pipeline because that varies based on the complexity of your type of sales. It might take multiple meetings to meet with all the decision-makers for instance, so opportunities might sit for a bit at that stage. Or you might have opportunities in one conversation that fly through the stages. The time doesn't matter; the *analysis of closing success* matters. This is a key differentiator between an effective pipeline versus the traditional pipeline that just has stages based on something that happened. This is why the pipeline needs to be constructed with care. And, if using a CRM, customize the pipeline so the salespeople are prompted to ask certain questions and know certain things prior to movement from one stage to the next.

Conduct the analysis. Determine the likelihood of success based on the different stages. Most likely many more opportunities get stalled in the "knowing why the prospect is talking with you and their need" than in the proposal-ready stage. If you don't know or cannot conduct the analysis to determine these closing percentages for your pipeline, do one of two things:

- Simplify the pipeline (you may have it too granular with too many stages)
- Apply guesstimate percentages to each stage until you can go back and validate it

A rule of thumb is that only 25 percent or 30 percent of opportunities are going to close from the first meeting, similar to a good baseball-batting average. Then the percentages will increase from there with a crescendo at the proposal-ready stage. But for this to be predictive, you must have hurdles or gates that must be met before an opportunity can move to the next stage.

And never, ever leave the closing percentage assignment up to the salesperson. You will have some that are pessimistic or superstitious, thinking that nothing is going to close, and some that are overly optimistic and think everything will close. So take this variability out of the equation and assign a standard closing percentage for each stage.

Validation is the key to ensuring the pipeline is structured correctly with the right percentages. Depending on your sales cycle, you may need to collect data for three months, six months, or more than a year to precisely calculate the closing percentages for each stage. But keep it simple in the beginning and tweak it as you go.

Having standard closing ratios provides you a window into understanding your individual salespeople. If you have a salesperson whose opportunities are frequently progressing through the pipeline but the opportunities are not closing at a rate consistent with the norm, then this indicates the need for some additional joint sales meetings, call planning, and coaching.

Pipeline discussions

The pipeline alone won't move opportunities along. As I suggested before, publicly going through each and every opportunity in a salesperson's pipeline is a common practice but is not that helpful. Rather, conduct those conversations in private during a one-on-one coaching conversation. Too often, when a sales meeting is taken up with sellers going through their pipeline, the same old names keep coming up with no movement. And it places too much emphasis on the pipeline as a repository where opportunities just hang out. If too much focus is on the number in the pipeline, then salespeople can be enticed into the bad behavior of just putting opportunities into the pipeline. The pipeline should help the salespeople know where they stand with an opportunity and determine what they need to do next. It should be more of a guide rather than a dumping ground of deals.

Depending on your business and the number of opportunities each salesperson needs to have in their pipeline (think Math of Success), it may be too time-consuming to go through each and every opportunity in the pipeline with each salesperson. So instead if you focus your attention on coaching the salespeople to have better qualifying (or disqualifying) conversations along the way, then you won't need to prod them on each opportunity. If time is limited and opportunities abound, have the individual pick out a couple or a handful of opportunities that they will move forward with this week. Help them plan out what they need to do to make that happen.

Additionally, in your pipeline discussions, ask each and every one what the next agreed-upon step is for all or a subsegment of the opportunities. The first step is knowing that there is a next step, and the harder and more important step is that the next step is agreed upon between the seller and prospect. It is a starting point that all opportunities have a next step assigned to them (easily done in most CRMs), but the more impactful next steps are those that the other party has actually agreed to. Rather than saying, "I need to call them back next week," a far superior and efficient next step would be that next week's call was actually agreed upon and set for a specific day and time. This sounds so much easier than it is; however, you, as their leader, can help them gain this discipline simply by asking, "What is the agreed-upon next step?" Do that consistently and frequently enough, and your team will start to establish the next steps.

Move them or blow them up

A reliable and predictive pipeline should be cleared out on an ongoing basis. Consistent with my message that just having opportunities in the pipeline is not healthy, you must help your salespeople gain rigor around clearing it out. Do not let them hang onto opportunities that are unlikely to close. Since salespeople often keep opportunities in their pipeline only because they don't have a good system to check in with those opportunities, make sure your process reminds the salesperson to check in with lost opportunities at a certain point in the future. Set up workflows reminding them to check in in two or three months to see if circumstances have changed. And better still, support them with marketing messaging that will keep your company top of mind with those lost opportunities until a time in the future when they might be more prepared to engage with your company. These two mechanisms will free up the salespeople to keep their pipeline clean and predictive.

You must be their accountability partner in this process, challenging them about the opportunities that have been lingering for too long. Encourage them to either move the opportunity along or blow it up and get it out of the pipeline. Just like a messy desk can cause distraction, a messy pipeline is distracting as well. It provides salespeople with a false sense of security. It may cause them to focus on these opportunities that might never close rather than going out and finding better opportunities. Demand that the pipeline not be littered with junk.

In conjunction with the use of a repeatable selling process, the pipeline should help a salesperson improve their efficiency and effectiveness if structured correctly and if you are coaching to it.

- Too much focus on the pipeline can cause bad behavior by loading up the pipeline with crap.

- Your pipeline should be very reliable and predictive of which business will close.

- Take care in designing stages of the pipeline that identify what your salespeople need to know to suggest a higher probability of closing rather than just activities they are performing.

- Be diligent in managing the pipeline along with your salespeople in individual review sessions, and require them to have an agreed-upon next step for each stage of the process ("agreed upon" being the operative words). Adopt the phrase "move the opportunity or blow it up."

- Create a workflow that helps salespeople feel comfortable removing opportunities from their pipeline because they know they will be reminded to follow up.

- Ensure each stage of the pipeline has an assigned probability of closing that cannot be altered by the salesperson.

Improvement Exercise: Analyze your team's pipeline over the last six months (or a year, depending on the typical length of the sales cycle) and validate whether the pipeline is truly reliable and predictive. If not, employ the changes suggested.

Conducting Inspiring Sales Meetings

"When leaders know how to lead great meetings, there's less time wasted and less frustration. We have more energy to do the work that matters, realize our full potential, and do great things."

—*Justin Rosenstein, co-founder Asana*

Sales meetings should be invigorating, inspiring, and fun, but too frequently they are boring, long, and dreaded. This is mainly due to sales managers feeling compelled to have meetings without being sure why or what to cover. Therefore, they just conduct the same sucky meetings that they participated in as a salesperson. We need to stop that vicious cycle of mediocrity. When I was first a manager, I got so nervous conducting the weekly meeting because I felt that I had to be the show. But sales meetings can be and should be an event that the sales team looks forward to each week.

Surefire ways to conduct valuable sales meetings

First, let's discuss the purpose of a sales meeting. It should be an opportunity for the whole team to come together, whether in person or virtually via a web meeting platform, weekly. Some organizations lend themselves to even a daily "huddle" because the sale is a fairly transactional, low-dollar amount and they expect multiple sales to happen every day, but I am not going to address that format here. Instead, I am focusing on the weekly sales meeting.

So how do you get salespeople to anticipate these weekly meetings with joy? They must be valuable to them, and they must be worth the time they spend away from selling to attend these. Engagement is the key to a successful sales meeting and one where the salespeople are truly finding value.

Let's explore what is valuable to your team:

- Receiving ideas or suggestions that can help them sell more (Any outsider that comes into your meeting must provide information that enables the sales team to go out and solve problems or provide solutions for their clients, not just provide data.)
- Getting help with difficulties that are preventing them from selling more.
- Feeling safe to admit that they don't have it all figured out (Some of the most valuable moments in a sales meeting include an individual sharing something they are struggling with and having the whole team rally around them to offer suggestions and ideas.)
- Being publically celebrated. (This *might* be good because if you think back to the chapter on motivating and goal setting, you may recall that some individuals don't necessarily need nor want public recognition. So, tread carefully. If there are opportunities to celebrate the entire team, that is fantastic. And if you have a team full of extrinsically motivated individuals—those that want and maybe need external elements to motivate them—then by all means, recognize those individuals that have outperformed or won a tough opportunity.)

Ideas for successful sales meetings

You may want to have a regularly scheduled meeting each week, but maybe one week out of the month is a longer meeting with a meatier focus. When my company works with clients, we like to take over one of their regular sales meetings a month because that makes it easier to keep the salespeople on the same schedule.

Regardless of your schedule, you need to be clear about the purpose for having the meeting.

And make sure you don't have a meeting just for the sake of having the meeting. However, do not skip or avoid holding meetings just because you don't want to put thought into the purpose and the format of the meeting. Regularly scheduled sales meetings that bring the team together can be very beneficial. Keep in mind what is valuable to your team, then consider including the following potential elements in your sales meetings.

Set expectations for the meeting. All meetings seem to work better when everyone is clear on how they are to operate. Set the ground rules, which could include:

- Only one person speaks at a time
- Nobody is allowed to dominate the conversation
- All distractions should be eliminated, electronic and otherwise
- The meeting starts and ends on time
- Everyone must have their camera on (if virtual)

Establish planned outcomes. What do you want your people to do or do differently as a result of the meeting? This should be clear in your mind, and you should probably communicate that to your team. Remember, keep the focus as relevant and valuable as possible.

Plan activities that allow for participation. If you have a team of salespeople who like to close business, then boring meetings where they don't get to participate may not be that motivating. Therefore, select some activities that will help them execute better:

- Everyone shares something they are especially proud of in their last sales week. They need to be specific and say why it makes them proud. You may want to ask questions about outcomes and what they did to cause the outcome so that others can learn.
- Everyone brings a "stuck" opportunity that they want help with or a challenge they are facing. Likely if one person has a situation they are struggling with, others do too. Remember, it is helpful for your team to be vulnerable and share the chinks in their armor. This is helpful to their growth and the entire team's. And the more you can get team members to help each other, the less you need to be the person with all the answers.
- Turn the above situations into role-play scenarios or plan other role-plays. They don't have to be long, drawn-out role-plays between two people, but you can have the team practice various aspects of the sales conversation. You can have people practice their "elevator pitches" or value propositions, or have them address the common objections your team faces, or practice how to discuss money, the ROI, and the cost of a prospect not doing something. Have everyone on the entire team coach and critique these mini-practice sessions. Although your team members may not love to role-play, and they may even protest, the more you can get them to do it, the better. And while role-playing one-on-one with you is great, doing it in a group creates more stress so it more closely simulates a sales situation, and the whole team can learn how others address these areas.

When asking team members to participate in activities, an easy way to enhance the engagement is to have each individual select the next person to participate once they have completed their sharing or role-play.

Before the meeting, consider if any resources or preparation is required. You may ask them to come prepared to talk about their most difficult situation in the past week, for example. Or come up with a call plan for an upcoming sales conversation. If you can, get individuals to think about the sales meeting in advance and how they will come prepared.

Consider rotating the facilitation. While you need to present sometimes, determine if facilitation could work better than your presenting to the team.

If you have a set meeting agenda, you can easily rotate the facilitation responsibilities across the team members, but you must be very clear about the agenda and stick to it. If you opted to have one meeting a month that is dedicated to a special training topic, you could ask one of the salespeople to train on that specific topic and present it. But make sure they are prepared and engaging. To do this, have them conduct a practice training with you first. This is a great way to help grow the skills of a team member.

What to avoid in sales meetings

Don't discuss sales pipelines. Sales meetings are not the time to dissect the pipeline. This is done in individual coaching meetings with the assistance of technology and your CRM. The danger of focusing on the pipeline in a sales meeting is twofold: 1) Certain salespeople will drone on about the same stale opportunities in their pipeline, bragging about how grand their pipeline is. 2) It may cause individuals to believe that the pipeline is the most important thing, taking the focus away from what is important: moving those opportunities to the end of the pipeline and closing business. Discussing pipelines is handled much more effectively in one-on-one coaching conversations. Now, if a salesperson is having difficulty with a particular opportunity, then discussing a plan of action in the sales meeting and soliciting advice from the team is a productive use of meeting time.

Don't have general discussions about sales results. It doesn't do a ton of good to state generalities. For instance, if the team is behind in their goal and you focus on this point as a collective problem, it can have unintended negative consequences. If the team is collectively behind their goal, likely one or more people are at or ahead of their goal, so they will either be resentful that the rest of the team is not achieving at their level, will rub it in others' faces that the problem resides with other people not them, or just be unengaged altogether. Additionally, the people who might be dragging the team results down may not even realize that they are the problem when this is discussed in a general sense in a team setting, especially if the team collectively is producing results. A lack of results is an individual discussion and should be focused on the behaviors and activities that an individual will change to produce better results. So in sales meetings, rather than focusing on the results, use a situation where the team is behind in their numbers to focus on a skill-building component that will help overcome the situation.

The time I do encourage you to discuss collective sales results in the sales meeting is when the team is crushing their goals. When everyone is hitting on all cylinders and sales are stellar, this calls for a celebration, which can be conducted in the meeting. Consider something different and special that all will enjoy if a challenge has been met.

Avoid product dumps, listing features and benefits. Too frequently sales meetings turn into a product dump, especially if you allow outside manufacturers in to hijack your meeting. Don't let other departments in your company take over your sales meeting to share administrative or operational information. That is not helpful unless the salespeople are requesting more information about a certain product or service to enable them to sell more of it. And in the event some product or operational training is necessary, make sure that the presenters are going to share information in a way that provides the sales team with what they need to actually sell better. Require any outside presenter to share the value proposition to your clients for the information they will present to your team. Have them share use cases and stories of what it has meant to other clients.

Use sales meetings to engage, energize, and push your sales team. If you put a little thought into it in advance, you can conduct meetings that help your team execute at a higher level, reduce the burden on you to "tell" everyone what to do, and increase the fun factor across the whole team.

KEY TAKEAWAYS

- Sales meetings should be inspiring and help salespeople execute their work more effectively.

- You, as the sales manager, do not need to be the presenter. Think facilitation more than presentation.

- Engage the team members in interaction and use role-play and practice as much as possible.

- The environment should be one where salespeople feel safe to show their vulnerabilities.

- Do not conduct pipeline reviews in these meetings.

- Focus the meeting on sales, not product information.

Improvement Exercise: Think about your typical sales meetings and determine if improvements can be made. If so, identify the areas that you will change.

Sales Process

"If you can't describe what you are doing as a process, you don't know what you're doing."

—W. Edwards Deming

Most salespeople don't follow a standard repeatable sales process. They waste time and possibly miss opportunities because they're not focused on the right opportunities. A repeatable sales process ensures they focus on the right opportunities, enables better coaching on your part, and improves the team's effectiveness.

A sales process is a repeatable, logical series of steps that includes milestones. It is a roadmap, detailing exactly what needs to be accomplished at each stop along the way. By following a logical progression, salespeople can perfect the skill of asking the right questions and getting the necessary answers needed to either close business or quickly determine that this isn't the right opportunity, allowing them to spend their energy with more likely prospects.

Similar to any other repeatable process in business, the idea behind instituting any process is to improve efficiency and accuracy. Many businesses seem to rely heavily on the skill of their salespeople rather than implementing a proven process that will improve results. While sales is an art, there is also predictability, and following a sales process is one of the easiest ways to improve sales. In fact, following a process doesn't really require any sales skills or any special sauce. It just requires discipline in following the steps.

While nuances and specifics exist for each company, the basics are similar, and any successful sales process includes nearly identical foundational elements.

Common elements throughout the sales process

Certain elements of the sales process should be established at the beginning of any sales conversation and should continue throughout the conversations.

Rapport building. Connect with the prospect in a manner that appeals to the prospect. This is *not* a one-size-fits-all approach. In the old days, salespeople were taught to notice the pictures or trophies on a prospect's shelf and comment on them. Not only is that outdated for today's combination of face-to-face and virtual selling, but it also ignores the fact that some people may not want to discuss their pictures or trophies with a stranger. An easy way to establish rapport is to do a little homework beforehand and determine what might resonate with the other party. People are unique, so your salespeople need to initially read the signals and build rapport in a careful way; then they must continue to deepen the relationship by continuing to read the other party. The key to building rapport is adapting to the communication styles and desires of the other party. But above all else, salespeople need to be genuine and authentic. They must adapt their communication style, but be themselves.

Establishing the ground rules. Establish the agenda and create an environment of trust and openness. Early on, the seller should position themselves as valuable and different than others. In an ideal situation, the seller should position themselves as someone the prospect trusts and maybe even admires. This does not mean dressing a certain way to impress. What it does mean is exhibiting confidence that they're a peer to the other party or a peer for this particular need. One of the most effective ways to do this is to establish a set of rules for them, which include telling the prospect to ask questions and to not string the seller along by saying "I need to think it over," but instead request the prospect says no if they aren't interested. I like to characterize this part of the process as setting covenants with the prospect. And it happens not only at the beginning of the conversation but throughout the process. For everything the prospect asks of the seller, the prospect needs to be prepared to give something back. So if the prospect requests a proposal, the prospect should be willing to schedule a time to discuss it with the seller upon receipt. Requiring the prospect to be a partner in the process elevates the salesperson from peddling their wares to becoming a peer of the prospect.

Sequential steps of a well-defined sales process

Step 1: Establish the fundamental buying motive. This includes why the prospect is interested in talking, why they are interested in talking now, and why with your company. It includes understanding what the problem is, what the issue might be, and what the goals of the company are, as well as the goals of the individual prospect representing the company. In this phase of the conversation, the seller should not only understand their compelling reason to do something about their situation but also uncover how compelling it is. If it is a nice-to-have as opposed to a must-have, they're not as likely to close. As the manager, you must help your sellers understand that just because they think the prospect needs what your company offers, the prospect has to feel that they need it too.

Step 2: Establish the financial impact. This is the ROI of your offering, but it is also the cost associated with not fixing their situation. This step is most impactful if you can quantify both the ROI for your products or services and the cost associated with the prospect *not* working with your company to solve their situation. Certainly, it includes their ability to pay for your services, so at this point, salespeople must discuss the prospect's ability to pay for what is being offered and their inclination to buy from your company. If your business is not responding to RFPs and RFQs exclusively, then likely your salespeople will need to introduce the need for your company's products and services, and depending on what you sell, your targeted prospects may not have considered purchasing your services, so they don't have the budget for it. So while some opportunities may have defined budgets, it is rarely valuable to ask, "What is your budget?" Rather create a series of questions for salespeople to use that help the prospect understand the financial impact of not fixing their problem. Certainly, if your products lend themselves to creating an ROI that can be calculated, then by all means do that as well. But if there isn't an obvious calculation, be sure to establish a process for asking questions about what the prospect's current state is costing them. And while it is fantastic if this can be quantified, do not discount the fact that stress, worry, fear, discomfort, and unhappiness are costly as well and can also be compelling reasons to change what they are doing.

Step 3: Understand everything about their decision-making process. The next step on the sales process journey is to not only understand who makes decisions of this nature for the company but also how they are made. While it includes understanding all the potential people impacted and their influence on the decision-making process, that isn't the full extent of it. How will the prospect know who the right provider is? How did they choose to do what they have been doing? Then from there, the salesperson needs to understand what it would take for the prospect to switch (if there is an incumbent) and what it would take for them to continue doing what they are doing. This is the who, the what, the how, the why, and the when. Few sellers dig into this beyond trying to find out who will make the decision. And, frequently, even when the salesperson is meeting with the person that they assume is the decision maker, or who has even indicated that they make these types of decisions, they are rarely the sole decision maker. In fact, according to Gartner.com an average of six to 10 decision makers are involved in typical complex B2B buying decisions.

Constructing the road map

Now that the components are defined, how do you construct the roadmap for your salespeople to move effectively and efficiently through the process? With questions. Engage your team in a question-creation project specific to your organization and your target market. Craft a laundry list of the best questions to get to the heart of each of these steps in the process.

Establish the Fundamental Buying Motive	Establish the Financial Impact	Understand Everything about Their Decision Making Process
Why are we meeting?	What is this problem costing you?	Who else do you bring in when making a decision like this?
Why are we meeting now?	If our solution costs between $x and $y does that sound reasonable?	What other options are you considering?
What have you done to try and fix this previously?	What type of ROI are seeking?	How will you know which provider is right for your company?
Are you being held responsible for fixing this?	What are the potential financial consequences of doing nothing?	Under what circumstances would you keep doing what you are doing?
What happens if it doesn't get solved?	What will it cost if you make the wrong decision?	What would have to happen for you to select us?

Some of these questions may be familiar from the pipeline discussion in chapter 7.

Realize, too, that the road may not be a straight line. In a typical sales conversation, these points may be brought up repeatedly, so the salesperson has to ebb and flow with the conversation. To help them do this, have a clear map indicating where they're trying to go. If they have a clear idea of where they are headed, then it frees them up to have deeper conversations and really connect with the other party.

This also helps with an issue that many salespeople suffer from: shiny object syndrome. Since many salespeople are social beings, they tend to go down a rabbit hole with a prospect and lose track of where they're headed. And, sadly, before they know it, the time is up, and they didn't make much headway toward the goal, which is likely determining whether there is a true opportunity or not. By mapping out the sales process, it can make it so much easier for these easily distracted salespeople to stay focused on the task at hand.

Disqualifying vs qualifying

Typically salespeople are taught to qualify their opportunities. This sales process provides a framework with which to do so. However, I suggest your salespeople focus on disqualifying their opportunities, rather than qualifying them. To do this, once you have created your laundry list of great questions, determine which answers indicate less success in closing opportunities. Maybe create a checklist of questions that must be answered to fully qualify an opportunity before a proposal is allowed to be created. If the answers to these questions are unknown, then the salesperson has to go back and get the answers. If the answers aren't favorable, then the prospect is disqualified. As I shared in great detail in the chapter about pipeline management, it is highly detrimental to allow a salesperson to believe that an opportunity is real if it isn't. If you can flip the thought process from qualifying to disqualifying, you will build more confident salespeople who are focused on the right opportunities and, therefore, will have more success.

By using this sales process, they can identify areas where the prospect may not fit.

Establishing the ground rules. If they aren't willing to participate in the process, so the salesperson isn't reduced to peddler status, is this really a prospect?

Fundamental buying motive. If it is just a nice-to-have for the prospect, then the salesperson needs to dig more before it makes sense to spend a ton of time trying to convince the prospect they need what you have to offer.

Financial. If they don't have the money or won't part with it, they aren't a prospect.

Decision-making. If it isn't clear how they will make a decision, more digging is necessary before spending more time on them.

Sales process coaching

If you can institute a repeatable, predictive sales process, your job will be so much easier as well, as you will:

- Know exactly what components to focus on when coaching your team members
- Have a framework for helping them plan their calls
- Have a template to follow during debriefing
- Be able to identify where a salesperson is weak in their conversations and where they need help

Using the call planning and debriefing templates provided in *The Happy Sales Manager Workbook,* found at thehappysalesmanager. com, makes it simple to focus on coaching them where needed.

Presume that they are following the process and ask them questions about the process. So rather than asking, "Did you ask them about their decision-making process?" maybe try something like, "When you asked them about how they will know who the right provider is, what did they say?" This can be a very powerful reminder of the diligence they need to take to follow the steps and conduct the most productive sales conversations.

Following a repeatable process alone should increase sales success, regardless of their sales expertise. The key is to ensure they are doing it and structure your coaching around it.

KEY TAKEAWAYS

- Many salespeople shoot from the hip in sales conversations, but a repeatable sales process will help your team close more business.

- Creating a sales process that incorporates the right questions to ask along the journey will allow the salespeople to have better, more robust questions because they won't have to think about where to go next with the conversation.

- Helping your team incorporate a mentality of disqualifying opportunities as opposed to qualifying will help your sales team stay focused on the right opportunities, which will increase sales success.

Improvement Exercise: Construct a framework for your sales process which will help your salespeople have a plan to follow in their sales conversations. This is a great exercise to have the team work on together.

Business Management

"There are no secrets to success. It is the result of preparation, hard work, and learning from failure."

—Colin Powell

Sales managers should spend 75 percent to 80 percent of their time on sales management, which means coaching, motivating, holding their team members accountable, and recruiting. However, there are other requirements of the position, such as reporting to your boss about performance, dealing with inter-departmental issues, participating in leadership meetings, reviewing compensation plan results, etc. So you will need to manage your time and make some room for business management.

Prioritizing your time

Just like with any role, you need to plan your time so you can focus on the most important aspects that will drive business growth. As your primary responsibility, you're charged with growing sales (and profit) through your team. Therefore, the most impactful activities you can engage in relate to helping your team execute better. But the annoyances of other business aspects sometimes take over. Too often sales managers get sucked into areas that, while important, aren't the best use of their time.

Prioritize your time around the team. If you want to become a world-class sales manager and have your team over-perform, you need to do this. To ensure you prioritize your sales team, make sure you schedule time to:

- Engage in sales meetings, one-on-one coaching sessions, and joint calls
- Review sales results and conduct an analysis of what is happening in order to be prepared for the coaching sessions and to hold your salespeople accountable for their planned activities
- Be available for informal coaching as needed, similar to a college professor who holds office hours to work with students
- Engage with each individual, and proactively reach out to check in (especially if you have a distributed virtual team or a hybrid team with some in the office and some not)

Schedule the other demands of your job. You have to be focused and precise in your blocks of time. For instance, if you need to review commission reports monthly, make sure you schedule a specific time each month to do so, without interruptions. Focus solely on that function. Knock it out and be done with it. Do not allow salespeople, or anyone else for that matter, to interrupt you. Many sales managers have difficulty balancing their other duties with the needs of their salespeople. If you can structure your week and month to allow for specific heads-down work, then you won't feel obligated to urgently react to your salespeople's needs. You basically want them to know that you're available at certain times (most of the time) and truly unavailable at other times. The drain on many sales managers comes from the revolving door of their office with a stream of salespeople. If you don't schedule adequate time to interact in a focused way with all your team members, then you may feel obligated to respond all the time. This will make your other non-sales-focused work more difficult due to interruptions and switching gears. Allow for the influx of salespeople questions and interruptions, but only at prescribed times.

Strategize and create your quarterly sales success plan. This plan is found in *The Happy Sales Manager Workbook* at thehappysalesmanager.com. Make it a commitment to attack each quarter with a fresh focus. Prioritize your high-level efforts based on importance and use the list below as a guide:

- Biggest problem preventing sales growth
- Biggest opportunity to grow sales
- Biggest threat to future sales growth

Set action steps and due dates. Reserve time each week to work on these quarterly topics.

After all, your mission is to grow sales, and you need to prioritize those aspects of your job that will enable you to effectively do that through your team. Always prioritize the big important items, then create your plan of attack for executing those priorities.

Managing your relationships with your boss and others

As the leader of the sales team, you not only need to manage your people, but you also need to manage your boss and your relationships with other leaders and departments in the company. Sales is different than other departments in the company, so you and your team may sometimes be misunderstood and the other department leaders may not believe that you and your team work very hard, as many believe sales is easy and just a lot of fun-making. Therefore, you need to manage others' perceptions. And you definitely need to manage what your boss is thinking.

As part of your week, you need to communicate with your boss. Hopefully, you and they are in alignment with the goals for you and your team, and hopefully, you fully understand your boss's expectations. But even if you think you know, take the time to be certain. Whether you have been in the role for a while or not, regularly schedule time to provide an update about your team and to get on the same page. Regardless of the sophistication of your company, its size, or the tenure of your boss—you, your boss, and your team will benefit from having meetings to get on the same page. Do not rely on your boss to schedule this. Do yourself a favor and schedule it for the two of you.

When you start these meetings, have a plan. Be as focused and precise as possible. You may want to construct an agenda and get your boss' feedback on the agenda and whether it includes the right elements to discuss. Some suggestions include:

- Sales results for a given time period and year-to-date, including discussion as to what is being done if sales are behind or have experienced a softening.
- Highlight any particularly strong wins and the elements that led to those wins.
- If you have any underperformers, share that information and what you are doing about the situation. If there is a time frame for corrective action, activities that you are requiring, your coaching focus, etc., share that as well.
- Share how you are doing with your coaching schedule.
- Highlight any particular areas of difficulty. If you need help with something, ask.
- Provide insight into the pipeline forecast.
- Ensure that you both agree with the go-forward plan, and ask for feedback about how you are performing.

In addition to your boss, you likely must navigate and nurture relationships outside the sales department. You must make time to engage with and get to know the department heads to ensure that when a problem does arise, you are not at odds. It is not unusual for a sales manager to view the world very differently than an operations manager does, but if you both have the same ultimate goal in mind—to benefit the company, the clients, and the employees—and you have established a rapport, it will make it much easier to work through an problems if you have this common ground. If your company operates in a system where you have regular leadership or management meetings with leaders of different departments, that is a good start. But depending on the nature of those meetings and your company's culture, these meetings may not actually enable you to develop relationships with other department heads. Be sure to nurture those relationships by grabbing coffee or going to lunch, to get to know each other on a more personal level. Since there may be occasional differences in vantage points from sales to operations, for instance, you may need to be the mediator to help solve a problem, and it will be much easier to do if you have established personal relationships with other leaders.

Institute a report reduction act

The first step in reducing reporting requirements is to understand which key metrics are necessary to support sales growth. Too often reports are produced and never looked at. Or salespeople are asked to report on items, but the information is not examined and used to drive sales. Any reporting that is done must be focused on driving sales, as opposed to just a report that reports.

In a perfect world, you would have a CRM that collects and produces data that helps you and your team identify the right behaviors and activities to produce more business and provides easy access to insight that guides operating decisions going forward. Oh, and this system would also make it supremely easy for salespeople to input information, keep track of what they need to do next with a particular prospect or client, and receive feedback on what is working and what is not. But you likely don't live in a perfect world, so let's deal with reality.

Simple reporting requirements. Keep your reporting requirements simple while also providing the insights you need to enlighten your salespeople about the power of understanding data. You really need just a few reports:

- Closed sales this month and YTD (collectively for your team and each individual), and how this compares to your team goal and their individual goals
- Gross profit of those sales
- Number of first meetings conducted each week, and how that compares to each person's goal
- Weighted pipeline value (assuming your pipeline is staged appropriately and highly reliable)
- Source of the opportunity/business (new account vs existing account and what the genesis was of each opportunity)

With these five pieces of information, you should be able to zero in on what is working and what is not. Additionally, this information should indicate which individuals need to pay extra attention to their accountability and where you should concentrate your coaching focus.

Save activity reporting for coaching. You might notice that activity reporting is missing from the list. If everyone conducted their Math of Success exercise, then they have committed to a specific number of first discovery meetings each week. They have also committed to a certain number of specific activities each week to produce an adequate number of first meetings necessary to ensure they meet their sales goals. This concept is addressed in detail in the chapters on motivation and goal setting, accountability, and coaching, but paying attention to the five suggested reporting items can help you conduct better coaching sessions. For instance, if they are conducting the required first meetings but nothing is turning into closed business, then you can look at the source of the opportunity and drill down on where they're spending their efforts to generate business. Maybe they're barking up the wrong tree.

Some activity reporting is okay. I am not opposed to a certain level of activity reporting, especially for newer salespeople. If you know that it takes 250 outbound calls a week to produce enough live opportunities, then it would be helpful for the salesperson to know that and to track it themselves. Likewise, if you have found that your team has the most success with closing business from a certain source, then you may want to add a component that measures that specific element per week. Essentially, track the activities that produce the opportunities. For instance, if you know that you close more and better business from referrals, then maybe you should track the number of referrals that are requested by each salesperson each week and establish a goal around this activity for each. Just be sure to practice and role-play what that sounds like with the team.

While most of your time should be spent on true sales management, you still must tend to certain business management aspects. But make it as efficient and focused as possible to allow yourself the opportunity to focus most of your time on true sales management.

KEY TAKEAWAYS

- The role of sales manager requires attention not only to your sales team but also to broader business matters.

- Prioritizing your time to ensure you focus mostly on your sales team will pay dividends in results.

- Managing the relationship and understanding the expectations of your boss require attention and planning.

- Excessive reporting can drag your success as a manager down and that of your sales team as well. Focus on the most important reports that provide the insight you need to successfully lead your team.

Improvement Exercise: Keep track of your time for a week or two, like an accountant or attorney would. Analyze where you are really spending your time and determine what you can do to eliminate wasted or non-productive time so you can spend more time focused on helping your team overachieve and less time on business management.

You and Your Beliefs

Up to this point, we have discussed the primary competencies and the tactical elements necessary to proficiently perform your job as a sales manager. But there is more to your role than the competencies. You come with a collection of thoughts, beliefs, and fears, making up your mindset. And, frequently, this mindset impacts your ability to succeed more than your competencies and tactical skills. Therefore, this section is dedicated to helping you recognize the mindset that either helps you succeed in your role or has a negative impact. Explore these chapters to help you understand what you might be feeling, and learn how to effectively deal with these important areas.

- Growing in This Job
- Is Your Mindset Stifling Your Success?
- Imposter Syndrome

Growing in this Job

> *"People will forget what you said, people will forget what you did, but people will never forget how you made them feel."*
>
> —Maya Angelou

Being a sales manager can be a thankless position. If you don't have the right mindset of helping to drive sales through the team rather than through your own sales efforts, you will have a harder time finding enjoyment in your position. If you're still too focused on yourself and your results, not on your team, you need to consider why you're even in this position.

In earlier chapters, I have shared the "how" of the role of a sales manager: what it means to coach, motivate, and hold individuals accountable; the process for hiring and onboarding the right salespeople; and how to conduct sales meetings and manage the pipeline, etc. But where the rubber meets the road is understanding your level of commitment to doing these things that may initially feel uncomfortable or may be difficult to do because you like to wing it. However, if you want to be a world-class sales manager, you have to work on yourself. Sure, you have this job because you show some promise in this area, have demonstrated prowess in the sales function, or have been pressed into duty because nobody else could take this on. But as they say, "What got you here, won't get you there." Therefore, you must embrace the fact that some elements of this position might feel uncomfortable in the beginning. But if you want to have the most success and the most enjoyment in your role, please consider focusing on yourself and your development.

If you have been in any type of management role before, you may already have the appetite for success in this role. But while management roles have some application to sales management, many nuances to sales management make this role more difficult. The people aspect is obviously a huge item. The reliance on your team to drive sales growth, which supports the ability of the company to employ people and deliver its products and services, is a heavy burden that cannot be taken lightly.

Find your why

Your role is critical to the success of the entire business. So, therefore, you must take on your role with gusto, and you must have a desire for the role in the first place. If you don't want the responsibility of the position now that you know the necessary components for success and ease in executing the role, you need to find your "why" to gain a desire. If you have a strong desire to be successful in this role, that is a great starting point, as this desire will help you thrive in the role, but desire alone isn't enough. An awful lot of people want something badly, but desire alone won't make it happen. They must also be committed to doing what it takes to achieve. And sometimes this is uncomfortable. You may witness this within individuals in your sales team. They may want to max out their commission, but they aren't willing to do the hard work to accomplish that.

Don't let that be you. You need to do the hard work, and it begins with asking yourself, "Why do I want this position?" You may want it for the title or prestige. You may want it because you see it as a stepping stone to a larger role. That is fine, but in my experience, the sales managers that have the most success with their teams and also get the most enjoyment out of the position have some element of wanting to help their team members have success. If your "why" is grounded in your desire to help the team succeed, and if you achieve a sense of satisfaction from knowing you can help others excel, you will more easily take on some of the less pleasant elements of the job, such as holding people accountable to the right activities or coaching individuals who are struggling to succeed. Can you be successful if you're focused only on the title or the prestige or see it only as a stepping stone? It depends on the effectiveness of the existing sales team independent of you. But with those "whys," you may not be able to influence the upward achievement of the team, and you can certainly have a negative impact on the success of the team. People know when you are in it purely for yourself and not for them. You can't fake it if you really don't care about the success of the individuals on your team.

Build relationships with team members

While I have shared much about the specifics of becoming a successful sales manager, I cannot reinforce enough the importance of the relationships you build with your team members. None of the items I have suggested regarding coaching, motivating, and holding your team accountable work very well if they don't trust or respect you. It may not be natural for you to offer praise. It may be hard for you to build deep bonds with people. But to truly be successful, you will need to adopt the skills of a good leader. Sales management is not just about the doing; it is also about the feeling. It is about the connection with each and every one of your team members. Remember, you may not connect with each of them in the same way, but you must connect with each of them. They must truly believe that you're there to help them excel at their job.

To have that connection, you must care about them. Your impact on them will be long-lasting, whether you're intentional about connecting with them or not. If you just go through the motions of doing the work, your team will know it and may feel disengaged, and you will certainly have had no positive impact on them. If you don't value them and the work they do, you will have a great impact on them, but in a negative way. This might sound touchy-feely to you, but it's true.

Think back to mentors, sports coaches, teachers, and bosses that you've had. Those that you knew really cared about you and your success are likely the ones you remember most. You might also remember those other coaches, teachers, and bosses that made you feel unseen, or worse unworthy. As a leader of people, you're in a unique position to leave a mark greater than just sales growth. You're in a position to change a person's life—not only the life of those that report to you but those of their families and their communities. Think about the impact you can have on your team members by helping them achieve their goals and feel seen and appreciated. Consider the confidence they will take along with them in all facets of their life if they experience success in their job, an elevation of their self-worth, and an improvement in their whole identity. Your sales team is not just made up of robots. They are not just salespeople. They are people. If you can do whatever it takes to connect with them genuinely and authentically, you will have a lasting positive impact. And as a side benefit, they will likely succeed at greater levels than they otherwise would, which, remember, is a core component of becoming a successful sales manager.

Avoid focusing on yourself

If you have attained your position as sales manager because of your success in sales, you may struggle to focus on the team's success rather than your own sales production. To grow in this job, you must focus on your team, and you can't do that if you carry your own quota or are being compensated like a salesperson. Both situations create a conflict for the manager. If you were a successful salesperson and still have a quota as a manager, it's too easy to focus on closing business, even if you want to fully embrace the mission of a sales manager. If the plan requires you to close business, then selling may feel like the path of least resistance. After all, it takes patience to help team members grow and improve, and you may feel the pressure of getting sales closed now. And if you are compensated on your own sales, the pull may be just too great, and you'll fall into old selling habits. Then it becomes a vicious cycle. If you're focused on closing business because the company needs it, then you won't have time to appropriately coach your team members, which means they won't improve in their abilities to offload some of the selling and closing burdens from you. This leads to you running on the hamster wheel to continue to close business.

This scenario is not good for you, not good for your sales team, and in the long run, is not good for the company. You will become stressed out and will feel guilty you aren't helping your sales team members more. They will languish, and more of the burden will weigh on you, and you will burn out. Or salespeople will quit because they're not getting the support they need to develop. They might even feel like they're competing with you, which is not a good thing. And then you are stuck in the quagmire of doing the same old thing and expecting different results. I think this is referred to as insanity.

If you're in this situation—having your own quota and being paid compensation— then you may need to have an honest conversation with your boss to discuss the longer-term plan. If your mission is to grow sales through the team, then you need buy-in from the top of the house. They need to be on your side as you develop your skills as a truly successful sales manager, and they need to give you time to impact your sales team. Most leaders and business owners that I have encountered understand the difficulties associated with this situation. They also understand the risk that their company is faced with if too much of the sales burden is on the shoulders of the sales manager. They should understand the need to change the dynamics. But also be prepared to set goals and expectations of how this is going to happen.

To grow in this job, you must focus on the team, not yourself, and you will need the support of the company leaders to enable this to happen. Be patient with yourself too. This might be completely new territory for you, so you may not get it right and may feel like you're failing. Learn from your mistakes and proceed. Do not allow the pull to be the sales manager in title only while really operating as a glorified salesperson weigh you down. You may find that you actually don't like the role of sales manager, but give it some time. Don't quickly snap back to super salesperson mode just because learning a new set of skills is hard.

- Sales management can be incredibly rewarding if you focus on the right areas.

- To be the most successful in the role and gain the most satisfaction and enjoyment from it, you must be laser focused on your team's successes, as opposed to on your own successes.

- Sales management is not for the faint of heart. It requires a human connection with each of the individuals on your team, and they can be messy. If you're not up for the challenge, your job can be highly stressful, less satisfying, and in some cases, harmful to the team and company.

- A key component of sales leadership success is gaining the trust and respect of the people that report to you. This is not dictated by your position but rather through the way you support, push, and interact with them.

Improvement Exercise: Be totally honest as you complete an inventory of why you want the sales leader role. If you enjoy coaching individuals and feel excited when they improve, fantastic. If you're willing to hold people's feet to the fire because it's the best thing for them, then you're on your way. And if you understand the power of connecting with individuals in an individual manner, then you have the basic components to be successful. If not, then identify one area that you must improve to accomplish your mission as sales manager.

Is Your Mindset Stifling Your Success?

Most sales managers were never really taught how to be effective in their roles. They learn by doing it and often just do what their former boss did. In today's complex and ever-changing environment, a sales leader has to adapt to the individuals on the team, to the changing marketplace, and to the evolving needs of the client. And this all starts with your mindset.

Since you're human, certain thoughts or hang-ups might be stifling your success in your role. So you need to identify some possible mindsets that may be hindering you.

Not having the willingness

Similar to salespeople, sales managers not only need the tactical skill sets of sales management, but they also need to have the right mindset to excel. Frequently, it isn't the tactical nature of the role that hinders success and, therefore, a sales manager's mission. It's what is going on between their ears, or in their heart.

The first element of success is having the willingness to do what is necessary to be the best sales manager you can be. Reading this book is a good indication that you're willing to succeed in your role. While this book addressed some of the tactical aspects, the more complex aspect of the job is how you feel about doing the necessary things.

It used to be that sales management, or management in general, was more of a dictation to the people reporting to the manager, and they weren't questioned. That has changed dramatically, and therefore, sales managers must be willing to continually grow and adapt. The word *agile* comes to mind. Much has been written about being agile in selling; well, the same is true for sales management. If you just want everything to be black and white or are the type of person that wants to learn what to do and then just do it until the end, then you may need to adjust your perspective in order to be successful and enjoy your role.

You must have the willingness to grow, adapt, and do whatever is necessary to help the team reach their goals. You cannot be stuck in the mentality that "this is the way it has always been done." One of the most valuable traits of a successful manager is adaptability coupled with a strong sense of mission and what the goal is. If you aren't willing to adapt, you will suffer in the role. As Brad Pitt's character says in the movie *Moneyball*, "Adapt or die." If you aren't willing to adapt, change, learn, and grow, no book can help you. Don't be one of those people who reads tons of books about their craft, but doesn't change anything they are doing based on the information. Is it going to be uncomfortable at times? Absolutely. Are you going to feel like you don't know what you are doing? For sure. But muscle through, just like you ask your sales team members to muscle through and build new selling skills and mindsets.

If you have some gaps, as certain necessary skills or mindsets make you uncomfortable, you must be willing to close those gaps. Regardless of your reason for being in this role, please remember to bloom where you're planted.

This requires desire and the willingness to do what is necessary to be successful. It requires an open mind and a zest for growing and adapting to the needs of your team and the marketplace. It requires grit and perseverance. With a strong why and a willingness, you can close the gaps in any skills or mindsets that you might not naturally possess.

Let's assume that you have the willingness to succeed in sales management, you're willing to do what is necessary to excel, and you're willing to learn the skills we have discussed in this book. But even then, you may not be aware of other problematic mindsets that either are already hindering your success or will hinder your success. These include needing to be liked, latching on to self-limiting beliefs, and having trouble staying in the moment.

Needing to be liked

The problem. Some sales managers are interested in coaching, are great cheerleaders for their people, and truly want their team members to be successful, but they cannot deliver tough love when needed. Sure, most people want to be liked, but in your responsibility as sales manager, the need to be liked by your team members cannot overshadow your focus on the mission at hand—success in growing sales. If you suffer from this mindset gap, you might struggle with letting a salesperson know they didn't do what they needed to. It might be hard for you to coach salespeople when corrective feedback is required. It might be difficult for you to let them know they either disappointed you or let the rest of the company down by not executing their planned activities. You can't hold people accountable if your need to be liked gets in the way. And accountability is a key element in helping salespeople succeed. Part of the solution is being laser focused on your mission of helping salespeople succeed and part is a focused effort on working on yourself.

The Fix. Practice difficult conversations in advance. Plan it out, just like you would ask your salespeople to plan out their sales conversations. Identify areas that might make it difficult for you to say what is necessary. Plan out how you will react when they are defensive or make excuses as to why they aren't doing what is necessary. By having a plan, you will be less likely to revert to your instincts, which will make it difficult to say things that might be hard for the other person to hear. Remember, the reason you are suggesting something is for their benefit, not to make them like you more.

Self-limiting sales management beliefs

Regardless of how you came to be a sales manager, you likely have certain beliefs that limit your effectiveness as a sales manager.

The problem. It is common to have certain beliefs about your role and that of your salespeople. It is not unusual to believe that the salespeople reporting to you will do what is necessary to perform well without your coaching intervention, inspiration, and holding them accountable. Some might call this optimistic, but I call it wishful thinking. If you have any of the following 25 damaging self-limiting beliefs, as identified by Objective Management Group, you are hindering your own success:

1. I don't need to manage my salespeople's behavior
2. I don't need to give recognition to my salespeople
3. I don't need to set personal goals
4. I don't need to debrief my salespeople
5. I don't need to know what motivates my salespeople
6. I can't let a salesperson lose a piece of business
7. My salespeople don't follow me
8. I don't need everyone to perform at their best since I perform at my best
9. I don't need to upgrade the sales force
10. Raising my people's self-esteem is not a high priority
11. My salespeople should watch me sell
12. I need my salespeople to like me
13. It's rude to ask a lot of questions
14. Prospects are always honest
15. It's not OK to confront a prospect
16. A thousand dollars is a lot of money
17. It's OK if my salespeople let their prospects comparison shop
18. It's OK if my salespeople let their prospects think it over
19. Prospects that think it over will eventually buy from us
20. Our prospects won't buy unless we have the best price
21. My salespeople need to make presentations
22. Any lack of results is due to the economy or marketplace
23. Any lack of results is due to the policies of my company
24. Any lack of results is due to our competitors
25. A personal tracking system isn't that important to me

You likely have a few of these, even if you aren't consciously aware that you do. And it's important to change these beliefs, as these all have detrimental effects. Your beliefs directly impact your behavior, which produces or restricts your success. Luckily, by reading this book, you may have already washed away some of these self-limiting beliefs, but some may still linger.

The Fix. Figure out a way to turn the limiting belief you have around to change your belief system about it.

For example, if you believe that your salespeople need to make presentations, then your behavior will encourage them to make presentations. You might even be tracking how many presentations they do. Please ask yourself if it is always necessary to make presentations, or does it sometimes become a crutch for your salespeople to rely on the presentation to make a sale? Then change your belief to presentations are necessary only after a prospect is fully qualified and only in certain circumstances. Repeat this mantra to yourself daily multiple times and then help change your salespeople's process around the necessity for presentations.

For another example, let's say you believe that you don't need to manage your salespeople's behavior. This is number one on the list because it is a huge problem that I see. I have discussed previously that effective managers don't just manage sales outcomes, they manage behaviors to help salespeople produce more positive sales outcomes.

If you identify with this negative belief, then you must also reframe it. Maybe think about it this way. "I need to manage my salespeople's behavior to ensure they reach their goals." Or if the phrase "manage my salespeople's behavior" is distasteful, maybe think of it a different way, such as, "I need to help my salespeople focus on the right behaviors to ensure success."

Overcoming these conscious or subconscious thoughts will take focus and dedication on your part. But it is important that you do.

Trouble staying in the moment

Since you're human, you're afflicted with the same problem that we all are. Your brain can go much faster than a conversation can occur. Therefore, it may be hard to stay in the moment. If you tend to be a problem-solver or a creative or have been in your industry for a while, it might be especially difficult to stay in the moment.

The Problem. This makes it hard to truly listen to what the other party is saying and what is between the lines because you may have skipped forward in your head. When you're helping them to create a plan, it can be hard not to chime in and tell them what they need to say, especially if they're struggling with the situation.

Just like salespeople need a process to follow when conducting sales conversations, you need a process to follow to help you stay in the moment for coaching purposes. One reason that you might get sidetracked and struggle to be fully present is that you have not allowed enough time to conduct a robust conversation, so you feel rushed, or you have already checked out and moved on to the next meeting you have in your head.

The Fix. Refrain from scheduling back-to-back meetings if at all possible. Allow enough time to fully focus on the individual and the conversation that needs to occur. Then because frequently time runs out when a process wasn't followed so the conversation takes a turn, think about the goal of any interaction before you engage with your salespeople. Consider the impact you want to have. Having an agenda for your coaching conversations will help. A suggested agenda is available in *The Happy Sales Manager Workbook* located at thehappysalesmanager.com.

To be clear, none of these mindset gaps are psychological problems. Frequently, they are based on history, such as how we were raised and what messages our parents told us. They take practice to change, but they all can be addressed. And if you truly want to be the best sales manager you can be, you will need to dedicate yourself to working on your mindset as much as your sales management skills.

KEY TAKEAWAYS

- The most successful sales managers have the willingness to be the best they can be and are willing to grow and change, to adapt.

- You may have subconscious beliefs or attitudes that may be negatively impacting your sales management success and enjoyment.

- Evolving as a sales manager from that of a salesperson requires a shift in mindset.

Improvement Exercise: Examine your own beliefs about what it means to be a successful sales manager. Do you have the willingness to shift your mindset about items that might be stifling your success but may be long-held beliefs? If so, turn your non-supportive belief into a positive affirmation or mantra and repeat it multiple times a day until your belief changes.

Managing Imposter Syndrome

Frequently, because salespeople and others are thrust into sales management with no training or experience in the role, we see timid managers suffering from imposter syndrome. They may lose their confidence because they moved from something they were really good at to this new position, and they haven't developed the necessary skills to be confident in their new role. But, remember, your manager or your company owner obviously identified skills in you and has confidence that you can drive growth through the team. You do need to establish what your boss's expectations are of you, and if you don't already know, ask them to share why they selected you for this position. It helps to hear what they see in you.

Promoted to managing former peers

You're now the manager of a team that used to be your peers, so you may feel a little bit queasy about that or feel a little bit nervous. It's great to be authentic and acknowledge that it's awkward for you and might be awkward for them, but you need them to understand that it's your job to help everybody on the team be the best they can be.

To overcome this type of imposter syndrome, you need to establish yourself as the manager in a comfortable way and go from being their buddy to being their "boss." This doesn't require you to fundamentally change who you are, but you may need to establish some ground rules for how you're going to interact with them, state that you might not be as accessible going out after work with them, and ask them for some grace while you figure it out. You really do have to focus on your job. Your mission is to help them be the best they can be by being the best sales manager you can be, not to be a pal with them or be one of them.

Start by establishing a stronger relationship with each of your team members. Set aside time to be authentic and just say, "Hey, I know this might be awkward" and realize that it can be especially uncomfortable if one of your team members had wanted your job.

Managing more experienced salespeople

Now you might even feel more awkward if you weren't the best, most productive salesperson on the team. It's possible that someone on your team had more success in sales than you have, whether you have been promoted from within or have been hired into the position from the outside. But here's the bottom line: if they were the best choice for the sales manager position, wouldn't they be the sales manager? You have other skill sets that your boss felt were more appropriate for excellence in sales leadership. But that knowledge alone may not stop you from feeling a lack of confidence if there are stronger salespeople on your team. You may think you can't provide them any guidance and coaching or shouldn't hold them accountable, but think about your mission: to help everybody on your team be as successful as possible while driving toward the sales goals and the growth goals that have been established. While certain salespeople may have a longer tenure than you or have more sales experience than you, your boss felt you have the talent to help the team. It takes a special talent to coach and lead a team of experienced individuals, to help get the best from them, and to banish complacency, which frequently sets in with long-tenured salespeople. The selling landscape is constantly changing, and adaptability is critically important for salespeople of all experience levels. If you focus on the bigger goal, not how you are feeling, then you should feel confident in your ability to execute the various skills and activities mentioned throughout this book.

Let's say you encounter a team member who is far more experienced and maybe significantly more tenured or older than you are. How do you approach those situations? Build a relationship with them. Understand what they're trying to accomplish in their life. Determine how you can help them accomplish those things so they can have greater success. You may have to clear the air and own the belief that you are doing your job to help them do a better job at theirs. And if you were hired or brought in because leadership needed the sales team to go a different direction, you might have a harder time getting these seasoned salespeople to change. They may resist change and they may not want to adapt to what they need to do. If this is your situation, you may need to part ways with a salesperson or some salespeople. This can be difficult, but if you keep your sights on the bigger goal, which is to help them be the best they can be, you will at least have peace, knowing that you were genuine in doing what you could to support them. You can't make anybody change. And if their needing to change is necessary to achieve your overarching responsibility, to accomplish the growth goals established for the company and your team as a whole, then you have to do what you have to do to accomplish those goals. You must put the goals of the company ahead of any one team member.

Sales manager not from sales

If you don't have a sales background but instead come from an operational background, this isn't necessarily a bad thing, and I actually like applying the concepts of operational talent to the sales team. I also frequently see branch managers or general managers of branches carry the role of sales manager. However, sometimes a manager with a non-sales background might not have immediate credibility with the salespeople on the team. If you are in this situation and don't have a strong sales background, the activities I have mentioned may not come naturally to you. Since operations departments are typically more cut-and-dried than the nuances that exist in sales departments and operations is more instruction based, you may fall back on just telling salespeople what to do rather than dealing with the messy part of sales management. If this is you, don't get frustrated by the fact that just telling salespeople what to do will not work. Hopefully, this book has given you the necessary guidance to address the key components to help you be more successful. Apply your process-oriented mindset but work hard to understand the mindset and other factors impacting the salespeople on your team.

If you don't lean into the sales management aspects of your job, I can almost guarantee that your sales team will suffer. Your team will have less success than you would like it to have, and you will feel stressed out. Please focus on the people. Hold them accountable to the right behaviors because it is for their own good. Coach them consistently and frequently, and remember that salespeople need motivation as well.

- You are in this role for a reason. Remind yourself of this frequently.

- Set expectations with former peers about how your relationship needs to evolve.

- Build relationships to help the team understand that you're there to help them accomplish their goals individually and collectively.

- If you're not from sales, apply your operational mindset to aspects of sales but realize that effective sales management is more about connecting with the people than it is about following procedures and policies.

Improvement Exercise: If you identify with any of these types of imposter syndrome, think about how this might be negatively impacting your coaching or engaging with certain individuals on your team. Create a planned agenda for how you will conduct a one-on-one meeting with those individuals that cause you to feel this way.

Go Forth

Congratulations on reading this book designed to help you not only tactically succeed in the role of sales manager, but also help you gain more enjoyment and satisfaction.

Begin your path to sales management happiness and excellence by initially focusing on the core competencies critical to sales management success: motivating and goal setting, accountability, coaching, and hiring and onboarding. Once you have developed those competencies, focus on the tactical elements of your job: your sales organization structure, the compensation plan, pipeline management, sales meetings, and the sales process. Follow the advice in those chapters, and you will be executing at a very high level.

Finally, if you desire to become a truly exceptional sales manager, gain maximum enjoyment and satisfaction from your job, and lead your team to blow the doors off their sales goals, then be sure to spend time on the important elements covered in the final chapters. While you must attend to the business management functions of your role, do so in a defined, disciplined, and time-bound manner. If you think you may be hindered by imposter syndrome, spend some time working on this within yourself. Pay attention to the subtle mindset gaps and predispositions that may be sabotaging your success in sales management, and connect with why you desire this position. If you're not initially onboard with all that you need to do and you still feel more focused on your own success, make a plan to grow into the job and focus more on your team.

Be sure to download the accompanying *The Happy Sales Manager Workbook* designed as a companion to this book so you can document your plans and create your own guide to success. It can be found at thehappysalesmanager.com.

URGENT PLEA!

Thank You for Reading My Book!
I sincerely hope you found ideas and suggestions to help make
your life as a sales manager easier and more rewarding.

I really appreciate all your feedback and
I love hearing what you have to say.
I need your input to make the next version of this
book and my future books better.

If you loved it please rate it with 5 stars.

Please take two minutes now to leave a helpful review on
Amazon letting me know what you thought of the book.

Thanks so much!

Gretchen Gordon

Don't forget to download *The Happy Sales Manager Workbook*
which will help you put these practices into action.

http://www.thehappysalesmanager.com/

Printed in Great Britain
by Amazon

39162875R00081